P9-CCV-353

A QUESTUS PRODUCTION

Friction: Passion Brands in the Age of Disruption

Text © 2017 Jeff Rosenblum and Jordan Berg

Published in the United States by powerHouse Books,
a division of powerHouse Cultural Entertainment, Inc.
32 Adams Street, Brooklyn, NY 11201-1021
telephone 212.604.9074
e-mail: info@powerHouseBooks.com
website: www.powerHouseBooks.com

Designed by Jeff Wagener, Kevin Barnard, Shari Eaton and Aaron Wolk.
Cover design by Jeff Wagener, Charles Cording and Kevin Barnard.

First edition, 2017

Library of Congress Control Number: 2016962999

ISBN 978-1-57687-836-1

10 9 8 7 6 5 4 3 2

Printed and bound in China through Asia Pacific Offset, Ltd.

FRICTION

PASSION BRANDS IN THE AGE OF DISRUPTION

Jeff Rosenblum with Jordan Berg

 powerHouse Books Brooklyn, NY

This book is dedicated to my beautiful family.
I wish I could have written you a book of poetry.

Acknowledgments

I had an incredible team that worked with me on every step of the project. I am eternally grateful for their hard work and dedication. I was truly the least valuable player on the team.

The Strategy Team

First and foremost, thank you to the entire Questus team and our clients for inspiring and educating me. I wish I could adequately express how impressed I am with you every day. Thank you to my business partner, Jordan Berg, for supporting and investing in this crazy endeavor. I love you, man.

The Design Team

Thank you to Jeff Wagener for leading the overall design and development of the book. Thank you to Aaron Wolk, Chelsea Moriarty, Debbie Dumont and Charles Cording for strategic design guidance during the critical early stages of book design. You established a great direction and taught me a lot. Thank you to Shari Eaton and Kevin Barnard for designing and developing the internal pages. In particular, thank you to Kevin for the great work on the final tedious steps of the journey.

The Research Team

Thank you to Chris Schulz, Leeann Heeralall, Nicholas Manluccia, Scott Fiaschetti, Brianne Bitcon-Tupa, Tyler Rosenblum, Kayla Rosenblum and Danielle Marchione for gathering more research than I could possibly handle. I'm embarrassed by the amount of incredible data and case studies you uncovered that I couldn't figure out how to fit in this story.

The Content Team

Thank you to Joe Shepter for help turning a bunch of rambling ideas into a cohesive story. I appreciate that you didn't laugh out loud at some of the early drafts. Thank you to Lori Paximadi, Chris Kelly, Jena Marchione and Sarah Figueroa for edits and advice.

The Emotional Support Team

Thank you to Mom, Dad and Mike for teaching me how to read, write and use business for a lot more than making money. Thank you to Joe and Janet for sharing your incredible daughter with me. Most importantly, thank you to my incredible wife and kids for supporting me during the early mornings and late nights when I should have been playing with you.

Table of Contents

Friction is the difference between the way things are

and the way they should be.

It's the big things that prevent us from being who we want to be.

It's the little things that prevent us from **doing what we want to do.**

Fighting friction provides a system for prioritizing opportunities. It provides a framework for creative development.

Digital technology completely disrupted the brand-building model that worked for the last century. Fighting friction is the new way forward.

In a world where consumers are bombarded with marketing messages every moment they are awake, brands need to find a new way to stand out, get considered, build loyalty and win evangelists.

Fighting friction enables brands to divorce themselves from legacy business models. It is a revolutionary approach to building unprecedented customer relationships and unparalleled financial performance.

or

Revolution

Great brands are built, not bought.

Welcome to the revolution.

When Yvon Chouinard graduated college, he and his friends called themselves dirtbags. They meant it as the highest of compliments. Dirtbags didn't care about capitalism. They didn't care about material things. They didn't care about anything except enjoying the great outdoors.

Yvon was part of the 1964 first ascent of the North America wall of El Capitan in Yosemite, using no fixed ropes. Over the next few years he spent countless months rock climbing. When he needed a break from rock climbing, he and his dirtbag friends went to the beach and surfed. That's it. That's all they cared about.

They cared so little about the finer things in life that they lived off cans of cat food, which they mixed with oatmeal for extra sustenance. They weren't even regular cans of cat food. They were the dented cans that they bought for pennies.

Advertising did amazing things. It took brands to places they'd never been before.

Even when you're eating cat food, you still need pocket money. So in 1957, Yvon bought an anvil. When he took a break from surfing, he pounded on metal until he invented new kinds of pitons that enabled climbers to tackle routes they could never scale before. Yvon originally sold them out of his car, but soon grew his company to a huge success. He no longer needed to live off of cat food.

Then one day in 1970, he was rock climbing in Yosemite and saw something that he had never seen before. There was a hole in the rock. A scar. At first, he couldn't figure out what caused the hole. But it tormented him.

Finally, Yvon realized what was damaging the thing that he loved the most in the whole world. It was the pitons he created. His invention was scarring the rock.

For a dirtbag, Yvon had become relatively rich from those pitons. He had more than enough money to climb and surf to his heart's content. But the thing that was helping fulfill his dreams was also hurting what he adored the most—the rocks he loved to climb.

When I first heard this story, it made me think of the equipment that corporations use to grow brands. Specifically, advertising. Like Yvon's pitons, advertising originally did amazing things. It made brands wildly successful and took them places they'd never been before.

But eventually advertising started to scar what brands love the most in this world—their reputation with their customers.

Yvon didn't try to solve the problem with his original equipment. He threw out the old designs and created new aluminum rock climbing equipment called chockstones. They enabled climbers to scale the rocks without leaving a mark. The clean climbing revolution was born.

Ultimately, his new equipment led to the creation of Patagonia, one of the world's most successful outdoor gear and apparel companies.

From the start, Patagonia used a revolutionary approach to virtually everything. Nowadays it's common for companies to have on-site childcare and cafeterias dedicated to healthy choices. Patagonia had both in 1984. In 1986, it first committed a share of its revenue and profits to environmental causes. It demanded the use of organic cotton in 1994, before most people knew what organic was.

This is core to how the Patagonia brand is built. Patagonia rarely uses traditional advertising. Instead, they use a platform that removes friction. They understand that to enjoy their products, their customers need a healthy environment.

So they donate to environmental causes, create content that exposes the damage that their own manufacturing does to the environment and print collateral that asks their customers to buy fewer products.

This spirit was exemplified in their revolutionary initiative that took over their website and marketing collateral. It had a picture of a new Patagonia jacket and urged customers in a giant font: "Don't Buy This Jacket."

By asking their audience to purchase fewer jackets, they could help reduce the amount of garbage from old jackets and manufacturing by-products from new jackets. This was not just a passing PR gambit. This was a friction-fighting platform.

Brands need tools that don't create scars.

The friction that exists for Patagonia customers is that the creation of outdoor gear actually damages the great outdoors. So Patagonia built a platform to remove the friction. They empower the audience through education.

In spite of doing things that seem contrary to their direct interests, their approach is working. Patagonia has never performed better. That's the power of removing friction.

Fighting friction works because the digital revolution fundamentally altered the relationship between brands and consumers.

Brands can no longer create scars and cover them up with slick ad campaigns. Everyone knows the truth and they know it in real-time.

Just as Yvon needed to create a new tool to climb mountains, brands need a new tool to build success. A tool that improves people's lives. A tool that helps brands prioritize how their resources are invested. A tool that leads to unparalleled financial performance. That's what happens when brands replace friction with empowerment.

This isn't a book about how to create a good brand or have a good career. There are hundreds of books on those topics. This is a book about how to create a breakthrough brand. A brand that breaks its addiction to advertising and creates an army of evangelists. A brand that cuts through the hype of the latest media technology tools. A brand that focuses on behaviors over messaging. A brand that empowers its customers and dominates the competition.

Brands that fight friction empower.

Not just
interrupt.

tw

Branding

Brands are defined by their behavior, not their messaging.

2.1

Friction kills.

Humans have had a rough understanding of friction since the Sumerians invented the wheel. Centuries later, Leonardo Da Vinci was the first to recognize that the motion of the wheel was ruled by mathematical principles.

In the 19th century, the military philosopher Carl von Clausewitz applied friction in a way that also applies to modern business competition. He defined friction as the difference between war as we think it should be and war as it is.

Some of the world's most influential and creative people work in marketing. They are excited about this change.

Now it's brands' turn. Disrupted by search, mobile and social technology, brands realize that their cozy relationships with customers are in disarray. People have stopped looking at traditional forms of marketing. They have technology to tune out the thousands of brand messages they receive a day. They're cutting cords. They're downloading ad blockers. They get annoyed at the little things and amplify it through their digital connections.

We need a new paradigm to confront a new reality. Removing friction provides a path forward. It creates a system for embracing transparency, engaging audiences, building armies of evangelists and unleashing unprecedented growth. It is the modern and long-term way to build passion brands.

Some of the world's most influential and creative people work in marketing. They are excited about this change. They see that there's an opportunity to conduct business in a way that benefits both behemoth corporations and folks living on Main Street.

Brands were previously limited to communicating through an 11-inch print ad, a 30-second TV ad or a 300-pixel banner ad.

The creative canvas is now virtually unlimited. Brands have the ability to create utility and tell stories in completely new ways.

They no longer need to interrupt people. They can truly engage them. Not merely to entertain, but to bring value and meaningful experiences to their lives.

Machiavelli wrote that it was more important for a leader to seem virtuous than to actually be virtuous. That's the old model. It's why the advertising industry has been known for obfuscation and duplicity.

With the fall of traditional advertising, brands now stand naked in front of their customers. This transparency frees marketers to make long-term investments that affect people in positive ways.

Fighting friction can be as simple as helping people cook a better meal, play a better guitar solo, sign up for better healthcare or have better control of their personal finances. Fighting friction is about relationship building. It's about brands authentically finding a place in their customers' lives.

These new frictionless platforms are not cutting into margins as one would predict. Instead, they are delivering huge financial rewards. They are creating a new definition of advertising. One that puts less emphasis on projecting the image of being great and more on actually being great.

2.2

Friction is critical because it provides us with the framework we've all been looking for. It's the roadmap. The why and the how.

Inherently, we understand that a consumer revolution has taken place. We recognize that technology has permanently altered the relationship between brands and consumers.

But this communication disruption has only led to business disruption. Every day, stalwart brands find themselves losing market share while upstarts have captured our collective consciousness.

Trillions of dollars are being made and lost while brands grasp for the newest media and technology tools, not recognizing that the strategic underpinnings need to change.

2.3

Brands spend billions creating friction.

Traditional advertising is based on a reach and frequency model, which focuses on how many people brands reach and how frequently they can reach them. While the industry has spent decades perfecting this model, it hasn't stopped to think what that frequency is based on: interruptions!

In virtually no walk of life are interruptions considered a powerful tool for building relationships. They are one of the least appealing forms of communication. They are rude. They are annoying. They shut down the audience's ability to listen. But they have been at the core of the industry's strategy.

The old model was reach and frequency. The new model is reach and empathy.

The future for building true passion brands is not about simply buying interruptions on various platforms. It's about creating meaning and value. This is a sustainable approach based on real leadership—not a continual search for relevance on yet another platform. It will work now and continue to work in decades to come.

Finding friction is only half of the equation. The second half is the exciting part. It's about replacing friction with empowerment. It's about brands moving people's lives forward one small step at a time.

The marketing industry needs to replace reach and frequency with reach and empathy. Rather than relying upon paid media to interrupt people and hope they care, the objective is to create content and experiences that are so powerful people go out of their way to participate in them and then share them with others.

Content and experiences that are so powerful, people are affected on a visceral level, building a true relationship between the brand and its audience. A relationship similar to one they have with friends. One based on open communication, loyalty and understanding. It's about getting the audience to truly care.

The biggest question in any business decision is: who's picking up the tab?

The biggest question in any business decision is: who's picking up the tab for all this? That's the easiest part of the equation.

Corporations spend billions each year on paid media for their reach and frequency model. The money goes to TV ads, pre-rolls, mobile pop-ups, billboards and all the other annoying crap that gets in the way of consumers doing what they want. The great irony is that brands invest billions creating friction rather than fighting friction.

Every new technological advancement—web browsers, social media, mobile applications—seems to bring with it a new excuse to create friction. Marketers keep making ads, and the audience keeps running away.

It's easy to call this insane, but the simple fact is that it's institutionalized muscle memory. Marketers keep doing the same thing because that's what they know how to do.

Right now, for example, the business world has gone gaga over Millennials because they're starting to have disposable income. They now represent $1.3 trillion in annual spending. But Millennials were raised in a connected, transparent world.

Let's dig into the changes taking place to understand why friction fighting is so critical. For years, advertising built brands, no question. Launch a product, advertise, people purchase, invest in more ads. Do it at scale, and a P&G is born.

The innovation that first gave consumers the ability to fight back against advertising was shockingly mundane. It was a piece of indexing technology known as a search engine. It had all the sex appeal of a phone book.

If we are in the early stages of a business revolution, the rise of search engines was the Boston Tea Party. It was a signal event that promised violent change.

Search engines shifted power from brands to consumers. They no longer had to watch jingles on TV to learn what new toys to buy their kids. They simply had to ask Google. Instead of being mildly helpful, interruptive ads became annoying sales pitches from people they really didn't trust.

The problem only deepened with the advent of technologies built for outright avoiding ads, such as DVRs, spam blockers, ad blockers and do-not-call lists.

But that's just the physical avoidance of advertising. What's worse is the emotional avoidance of ads. Up to 89 percent of TV ads are ignored according to recent ethnographic studies—and not because of DVRs or remote controls.

The audience simply looks down at their mobile devices. They mess around on Instagram and email for a few minutes and look back up when the ads are done running.

In this model, advertising still has a core role. An empowering experience without advertising to build awareness is like a candy store in the desert.

But TV isn't the only casualty. Most marketers regard 2015 as a watershed, because that's when brands finally woke up to the fact that their customers were not sitting around watching TV commercials anymore. So they shifted the bulk of their money toward digital. 30-second TV spots became 30-second pre-rolls. Print ads became banner ads. Junk mail became spam.

Think about it: Digital has fundamentally changed the way that human beings interact with the world around them. And what was the business world's response to this world-changing technology? Pop-up ads. Motherfucking pop-up ads.

It's no surprise to find out that they aren't working. Data proves that you're mathematically more likely to survive a plane crash than click on a banner ad.

That's because the new interruptive ads are even more annoying than the old ones. Digital media has changed the way we look at the world and our expectations of how quickly things should happen.

In this model, advertising still has a core role. An empowering experience without advertising to build awareness is like building a candy store in the desert. Advertising must be used to generate traffic. But it simply needs to provide a gateway to immersive experiences. It no longer needs to tell the complete brand story.

Brands need a shift in strategy that is commensurate with the shift in consumer behavior. We're asking advertising to do too much. That's why the new branding model is empowerment over interruptions.

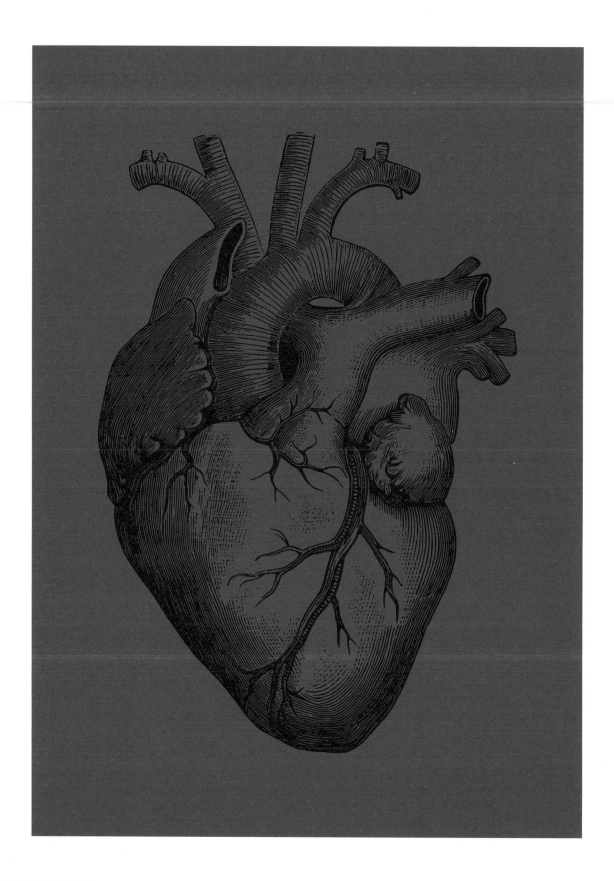

Removing friction shifts brands from transactional to emotional.

Transactional brands offer the right product at the right price at the right time. They launch ad campaigns that capture the audience's attention. People pay a fair price, they are not particularly loyal, and the relationship is completely rational.

Emotional brands, on the other hand, create irrational relationships—irrational in the most positive ways. They generate irrational enthusiasm. They charge irrational prices. They have customers who ignore the competition. They have evangelists who proselytize with clothing, online reviews and impassioned conversations around the dinner table.

Good brands are transactional. Great brands are emotional.

The best way to understand the power of an emotional relationship is to simply look at someone you love, like your children. Sure, your kids are extremely cute. But nobody gets more pleasure out of their photos and their videos than you.

The relationship that you have with your children is not rational, it's emotional, and that's a beautiful thing. They look better to you than to anybody else. They're cuter to you than to anybody else. They're funnier and smarter and more entertaining to you than to anybody else. That's the power brands have when they shift from a rational, transactional relationship to an emotional relationship.

You know who some of these brands are: SoulCycle, Apple, Patagonia, Under Armour. At this point you may be sick of hearing about them. But irrational brands are popping up in the most surprising of categories.

Take Yeti coolers, for example. They charge $650 for a cooler. Sure, they make a much better cooler than the competition, but they charge ten times as much as needed for a decent product.

It's not just that their customers happily pay this amount; they consider it a point of pride. As crazy as this sounds for a company that makes coolers, Yeti is a full-blown lifestyle brand. Those who can't afford a Yeti cooler will proudly purchase a Yeti hat.

While rational brands purchase 30-second interruptions and hope to God that somebody actually watches one, Yeti has a series of videos that extoll the virtues of outdoor adventures ranging from kayaking to fly fishing. They've been watched and shared millions of times over. Rather than simply sell products on the Yeti website, they use it as a storytelling platform. The site has dozens of the most inspiring stories I've ever seen.

In the videos, the Yeti brand is almost invisible. In one video about a death-defying all-night kayaking trip called the *Texas Water Safari*, they feature everyday people who push themselves to the breaking point for the sake of winning a patch that has no financial value and no bragging rights outside of a small group of fellow competitors.

The video is absolutely mesmerizing. With small cameras mounted on the kayaks, Yeti captures the thrill and danger of the event. It's unlike anything most people have seen before. It captures viewer's attention for a full 7 minutes. By comparison, the typical interaction with a digital ad lasts 1.6 seconds.

The only time the Yeti brand is clearly displayed is at the very end of the video on the hat of a competitor who passes out in the grass after the event. The product placement is fun, authentic and completely frictionless.

What Yeti proves is that removing friction is not only about taking away problems in the interactions that a brand has with its audience. It's about providing value throughout the entirety of the journey that people go through in life.

Yeti makes coolers that are certified grizzly bear–proof. Seriously, there's an organization called the Interagency Grizzly Bear Committee, and it endorsed them. That's clearly a piece of friction for those who are camping and fishing in very specific areas. But the greater piece of friction is that people desperately want to be inspired.

Yeti fans don't just watch the videos to be entertained. They are thought-provoking. They are motivating. They help Yeti fans envision a better version of themselves, one that is more active. More adventurous. More fun.

Rapha is another brand with seemingly irrational behavior that is creating irrational results. They charge more than $200 for a cycling jersey. That's four times as much as most other jerseys.

Rapha customers don't just happily buy the jerseys. They flaunt them. The brand is a badge. It's a source of pride.

Yes, they create very high-quality clothing and gear, but their customer loyalty is driven by something much bigger. Rapha focuses on enriching the cycling community. Rapha fans are not just looking for a great ride. They want to be part of a group of passionate, like-minded individuals.

The need for belonging is one of the most basic of all human instincts. Rapha customers don't just want to ride their bikes. They want to share stories and experiences. They want to push and be pushed to greater levels of performance. They have an insatiable need to be immersed in cycling culture.

So Rapha retail stores don't just sell products; they serve food and drinks and provide communal tables where riders can meet and greet each other. They are places where riders can tell tall tales and feel, innately, like they belong. Rapha helps riders get more out of cycling than simply exercise or transportation.

But the true beauty of Rapha's ethos can be found in the little ways they fight friction.

For example, they realized that many of their shoppers take a bike to the store, and most of these bikes are expensive. So they've built bike racks inside the store rather than out front. That type of behavior at face value is irrational.

Their location in New York City is one of the most expensive retail locations on the planet. And yet they're using space to give people a place to put their bikes rather than using it to sell products. It's unprecedented and absolutely not needed. But it shows a deep-rooted understanding of the audience. It demonstrates respect. It builds trust.

It's easy to dismiss the lessons of Yeti and Rapha because they compete in the outdoor category. There will always be something implicitly cool about outdoor adventure. But emotional brands can be built in the most unlikely of places.

USAA is a financial services firm for military personnel and their families. The friction that USAA removes is that people want more control and earning power from their personal finances, but ironically, most financial services do the exact opposite. USAA, on the other hand, makes transparency and control key performance indicators.

Recently I received a call from USAA. To be honest, I was barely paying attention. I was just listening to make sure I didn't miss a payment. Since it was USAA, I was willing to semi-listen.

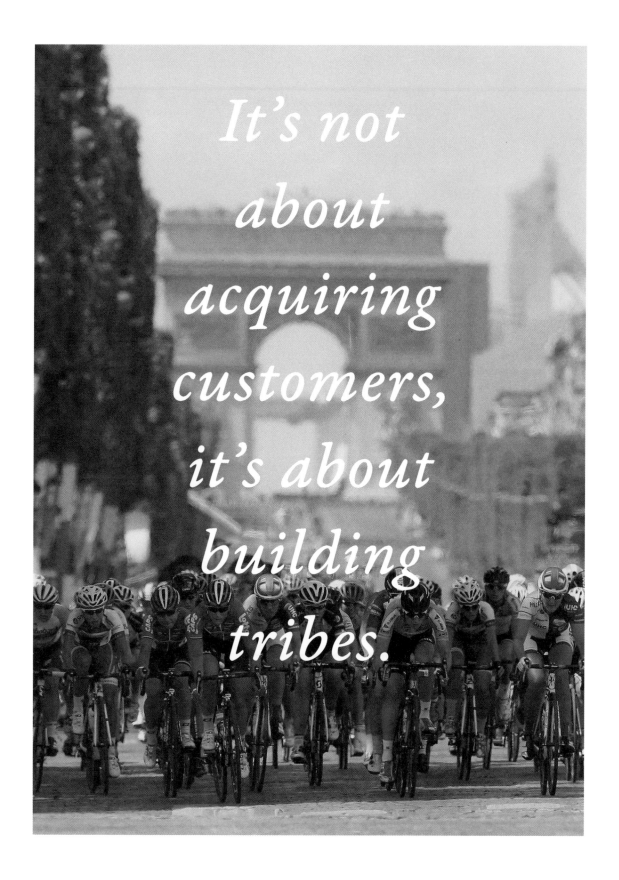

It's not about acquiring customers, it's about building tribes.

After a few minutes, I realized something and interrupted. "Wait, are you calling to tell me you are giving me money back?" I asked. "Yes, sir" was the reply in a sweet Southern drawl. Apparently, I had two different products with some crossover. They realized I didn't need them both, adjusted my account, and gave me money back. The total was $176. That's not chump change, but it's not life changing either.

What was changed, however, was my permanent perception of the company. As I go through the stages of life, I will consider and trust USAA before any other financial services company.

That doesn't make me unique. 92 percent of USAA members plan to stay for life. That's an insanely high number, particularly given that loyalty is often the most important predictor of business success.

Loyalty isn't simply a goal for USAA. They structure every aspect of their business to build loyalty through empowerment.

One quarter of its annual hires served in the military or come from a military family. They offer free financial advice to those being deployed or returning to civilian life. Their Educational Foundation conducts close to 850 financial management presentations annually to 50,000 attendees in the military community.

Despite the fact that USAA is fundamentally smaller than the competition, they've been leading innovators. They created an app that enables members to make deposits simply by taking a photo of a check.

While this technology is commonplace now, USAA owns the patent. They developed it so that overseas military personnel could remove the friction of depositing checks from the opposite side of the world. That's not just technology. That's empathy, empowerment and respect.

Looking back on the last 100 years of advertising literature, most people consider brands a promise or a story. That's insufficient. Ultimately, brands are a shortcut. Consumers are now bombarded with thousands of marketing messages every day. That's more than any human being can manage. They need shortcuts. They need brands they can relate to. Brands that inspire them.

So Yeti's videos about outdoor adventurers, Rapha's indoor bike rack and USAA's customer service may not seem like much. But they help turn those brands into shortcuts. The audience knows that if the brand understands them at a fundamental level, then it's a brand they can have a relationship with. It's a brand they can fall in love with.

We all have an innate desire for improvement.

When brands empower, thousands of years of evolution naturally pull the audience to those experiences.

thr

Categories

Macro friction is at the category level.

Micro friction is at the brand level.

As in economics, friction can be categorized into macro and micro.

Macro friction sits at the category level. It's the gap between the way things are and the way they should be in an entire industry. Removing it helps people have better vacations, gain better control of their finances or become better musicians. It helps people become a better version of themselves. Removing macro friction creates an emotional connection to a brand.

Remove macro and micro friction to create emotional and rational connections.

By contrast, micro friction sits at the brand level. It's not the big-headline, empowering stuff. It's the difference between the way things are and the way things should be in how brands sell and support products. It's anything that makes it hard to make the right purchase decision or get the most value out of products that are already purchased. Removing micro friction creates a rational connection to a brand.

To understand the difference between macro and micro, let's look at Uber, since it's a brand we all use and understand. The macro friction is that millions of people need a more convenient tool for short-range travel. So they created a safe, easy, reliable way for people to get a ride. Both drivers and riders simply need to use a straightforward mobile app. That's what removes macro friction. They elevated an entire category.

Yet, it's the micro friction aspects of the experience that are equally powerful. It only requires one click to provide your home address or share your music playlist with the driver. You never need to take out your wallet to pay, and you don't need to calculate the tip. What I find truly fascinating is that both drivers and riders are extremely nice to each other because they are policed by the five-star ratings.

It's the granular micro friction–fighting tactics that make it such an appealing experience. The user base for Uber is so passionate that the only advertisements you see for the brand are to recruit drivers to keep up with the consumer demand. That's the power of removing both macro and micro friction.

Remove macro friction by empowering people to get more value out of a category.

Let's dive deeper into macro friction. Patagonia removes it by fighting the ironic aspect of the category, which is that manufacturing products to enjoy in the great outdoors actually harms the great outdoors. Take, for example, those amazing board shorts that dry within minutes of getting out of the ocean. Mother Nature didn't make those shorts. When Patagonia makes those, it creates by-products, some of which are harmful to the environment.

So how does Patagonia manage this friction? Not by refusing to make board shorts, but by empowering intelligent choice. It created a tool called the *Footprint Chronicles* that shows customers the entire supply chain for its products so that customers can find out how Patagonia products impact the environment and what Patagonia is doing to improve. This empowers customers to decide if they want to buy or not, without the hype or obfuscation of marketing messages.

This isn't simply a campaign. It's part of a platform. At the moment that I sit writing this chapter, the first panel of their current website's home page isn't gear or apparel. It's a book called *Patagonia Tools for Grassroots Activists: Best Practices for Success in the Environmental Movement.* In their retail stores, they have bookshelves dedicated to similar content. They also produce documentary films that they promote through every possible channel they own and screen in their stores.

They use every touchpoint between the brand and the audience to hammer home a single point: We need a healthier environment. Patagonia is clearly passionate about the great outdoors. That's core to their culture. But it's also good business, because removing macro friction creates an army of evangelists that carry the brand forward much more effectively than paid advertising.

When I go fly fishing, it's shockingly consistent how heavily the guides are covered in Patagonia labels. By definition, those guides are the most influential people on the river. And you're damn right that people are influenced to purchase what the guides wear.

Interestingly enough, as Patagonia became a massive success, other brands misinterpreted the results and tried to be green, too. That's not the point. People don't expect that, and they don't reward it. They don't wake up in the morning expecting brands to hug the trees and save the manatees. Coke is out saving polar bears, but no one actually thinks Coke really cares.

Rather, this is a relationship story. Brands speaking to the audience in a way that's never been done before. Enriching people's lives in a relatively small but authentic way.

Patagonia's key competitor, The North Face, demonstrates this point brilliantly. It competes in the same exact category, but it tackles a completely different source of macro friction. The North Face realized that to fully enjoy the outdoors requires intense training.

They have Mountain Athletics, which is a series of training events led by experts that take place rain or shine. They have a speaker series where the audience gets inspired by tales from some of the world's great adventurers, and they fund nonprofits to enable the next generation of outdoor explorers.

Some of North Face's content and tools have changed over time. I was enamored with a series of North Face training videos that feature the world's best athletes in sports such as rock climbing and skiing. Apparently, they didn't catch on as the brand hoped, so the videos are less prominent.

But that's the beauty of an empowering platform rather than a campaign. The core philosophy lives on in perpetuity while the individual activations morph and optimize.

The key to removing macro friction is that it elevates the entire category, regardless of whether the people using the content are customers of the brand that created it. Patagonia's environmental platform helps anyone interested in the health of the planet. The North Face's performance platform helps anyone interested in outdoor fitness. It certainly appears unfocused to invest in content that could be used by a competitor's customers, but the point is to prove at an instinctual level that the brand truly cares about its positioning and its customers.

You can find macro friction in any category. It's why products and services are developed in the first place: to solve problems and fill a need.

But consumers want more than products now. They want experiences. Not arbitrary experiences. Not simply fun or entertaining experiences. They want experiences that move their lives forward, one small step at a time.

Remove micro friction by making products easier to purchase and use.

Only half the equation is removing macro friction. Admittedly, it's the fun half. Removing micro friction is the more rational but equally important component of the equation. Micro friction sits at the brand level. It is anything that impacts someone's ability to purchase or use a product.

It's everywhere. It's the plastic packaging that requires a machete to open. It's the instruction manual that requires a Mensa genius to comprehend it. It's the airline boarding pass that requires a magnifying glass to find the gate number. It's the telephone support that leaves a caller on hold indefinitely. It's the person behind the counter who doesn't smile when asked a basic question.

Fighting micro friction has increased in importance because the relationship between brands and consumers has become increasingly complex.

Not long ago, there were primarily two key touchpoints between a brand and its audience: advertising and retail. Brands like The Gap could develop a clean, organized, bright retail environment with relatively cool products and dominate the competition.

Now, there's an almost infinite number of ways that brands touch consumers, and most of them are digital in nature.

This digital-centric relationship has created exponentially growing sources of micro friction. It can be found on the website that isn't optimized for mobile, in videos that take too long to get to the point, in the hidden ratings and reviews, in the confusing error warnings, in clumsy checkout processes, in pop-up windows, in failed log-ins, in malfunctioning voice recognition replies, and thousands of other places that create stress.

We are witnessing entire industries being revolutionized by brands that remove macro and micro friction. Take restaurants for example. The macro friction is that food should nurture, but oftentimes it simply makes us unhealthy.

So brands like Sweetgreen offer completely organic meals that are served as quickly and conveniently as fast food. But it's the micro friction–fighting tactics that bring the macro friction platform to life. There is virtually no friction in the entire experience.

The containers are completely recyclable. You can't buy bottles of water, but they'll give you a cup for free water. There's information about calorie counts and food sources. You don't even need to wait online. Their mobile app enables users to place orders and pick them up at predetermined times with complete meal customization.

One might think this is some elitist brand that doesn't represent mainstream users. When I sat down to conduct research with customers at one of their locations to discuss this exact topic, a maintenance worker from my building walked in to pick up the lunch he ordered on his app. I'll take that as a pretty strong data point coupled with some ironic timing.

Consumers have too many options to have patience with a bad brand relationship. If they run into headwinds, they can quickly shift to a different brand or merchant.

It only requires one simple click for users to abandon a brand and less than a minute at the keyboard to bitch about their experience to millions of others.

Removing either macro or micro friction will make a good brand. Removing both creates a passion brand, one with a user base that is not only loyal but actively proselytizes. It doesn't work to fight one without the other, because each depends on the other.

Removing macro friction without addressing micro friction will make the brand seem inauthentic. Removing micro friction without addressing macro friction will fail to make an emotional connection.

People are bombarded with brand messages every moment they're awake. Decisions are made in seconds. People read social posts, not Shakespeare. All this has changed the way brains function.

Human beings are not patient. They don't need to be. There are too many new start-ups that focus on removing friction through digital tools. There are too many competitors in any category. Removing macro and micro friction is not only about creating a passion brand, it is critical for survival.

It doesn't matter what category you are in, Uber is your competition.

Customers have no empathy for your brand.

They only have heightened expectations.

fou

Results

Fighting friction has a massive impact on the bottom line.

How do we know it works?

The marketing industry is headed in the wrong direction, and the reason lies in one of the great plagues of the modern business world: metrics.

Of course, in many ways, metrics are great. They help separate the winners from the dogs in almost all aspects of business competition. But our greatest strengths are often our greatest weaknesses. Metrics have also been bastardized, abused and overused to the point of impeding forward momentum.

Metrics made the industry go ape shit.

Need proof? Look at your Facebook wall and see the never-ending stream of kitten pictures and other dreck that brands put up in hopes of eliciting "likes" and boosting engagement metrics.

Let's stop for a moment and see why this is such a problem. In its essence, marketing has only one purpose: to ethically help brands sell more profitable products. The only metrics that really count in that equation are market share and profitability.

But bottom-line financials take a long time to produce. Run a TV ad in January and it could take until April to get data about product sales. And it's almost impossible to tie that data back to specific advertisements.

So marketers created metrics to help themselves be more nimble. They found a correlation between short-term metrics and long-term financial performance, which allowed them to focus on things they could measure and control in the short term.

Among the first (and still most useful) metrics was gross ratings points (GRP). Basically, GRP measures the number of times an audience is exposed to a paid advertisement.

This creates a common platform for media negotiations and is a great tool for maximizing return on investment. For decades and continuing today, we can see a direct correlation between GRP and product sales. As GRP increases, so does revenue. But things soon went ape shit.

With every new media technology, the industry created more metrics to demonstrate success. The tail began to wag the dog.

With every new media technology, the industry created more metrics to demonstrate success. Web browsers went mainstream in the mid-90s, and with them came banner ads and pop-ups. With these ads came new metrics, like click-through rates.

At that point, the tail began to wag the dog. Instead of trying to help or support consumers, brands desperately sought ways to get them to click.

A decade later saw the arrival of social media, and the scene repeated itself. Brands now had a new set of readily available metrics, such as friends and likes, neither of which correlate to much of anything.

But brands nonetheless did everything they could to increase their audience and maximize the number of likes on each post.

Now with every new platform—Instagram, Snapchat, YouTube, Twitter and the five new social platforms that were developed while I wrote this paragraph—the approach remains the same.

Rather than focusing on providing consumer value, brands are trying to move metrics that have no proven impact on the bottom line.

So how do we know what really works? How do we know that fighting friction has a long-term effect on financial performance?

We stepped back to conduct a meta-analysis using both our own research and three large third-party studies. We also reviewed scores of research findings and bottom-line metrics.

Repeatedly, we saw brands that replace friction with empowerment outperform the competition by orders of magnitude.

Admittedly, we began our analysis in an unscientific way. We made a documentary called *The Naked Brand*. It told a story about corporations embracing transparency and building brands through holistic behavior, not messaging.

We expected it to be a controversial film that would piss off half the industry. Instead, it hit a massive chord. After an initial screening at the New York Times Theater, a woman ran into my arms crying and said it was the story she had been looking for.

She mentioned that she always loved the creativity of marketing, but knew there had to be a higher purpose to it all. I enjoyed the hug, but my overriding thought was that the woman was absolutely bonkers. After all, who cries after seeing a documentary about business behavior?

But the scene repeated itself again in San Francisco and Toronto. Admittedly, it was only a few people driven to tears, but clearly the story was resonating. In spite of our humble expectations for the film, demand soon carried it around the world to places as diverse as Singapore, Dubai and Madrid. In each city, the positive response was almost universal.

Clearly, we were on to something. Months after releasing the documentary, however, we realized we had a big hole in our story: we never actually checked to see if our ideas worked. All of our data was anecdotal, not financial. We got hugs and praise, but we lacked quantitative metrics.

And so, we created the Naked Index. We wrote down every company in the film and augmented the list with more companies that focused on empowerment over interruptions.

We didn't look for perfect companies. They don't exist. Just companies we felt were strong examples. We also limited ourselves to public companies so that we could access financial data, with stock price as our key performance indicator.

Next, we found comparable companies in the competitive landscape that didn't follow the same empowerment strategy. What we found was astounding.

Many of the selected companies had outperformed the competition as much as 10 to 1 over a 10-year period. 10 to 1!

The Naked Index's sample size was too small to be anything more than directional, so we looked for more substantial data.

Soon, we came across what would become one of our favorite pieces of research, a book called *Firms of Endearment*. In it, Raj Sisodia, Jagdish N. Sheth and David Wolfe studied companies that focused on holistic empowerment.

To reach their findings, they inverted Jim Collins's famous *Good to Great* model. Rather than identify brands that outperformed the marketplace and then work backward to understand key behaviors, they started with the behaviors and then tested financial performance.

Specifically, they reached out to business leaders, marketing professionals, MBA students and about 1,000 consumers to build a set of hundreds of candidate companies. They culled it down to 30 Firms of Endearment (FOE) that met key behavioral criteria.

Then, and only then, did they analyze the financial results. Again, they found something extraordinary. Not only did these companies outperform the Dow 8 to 1 over a 10-year period, but they beat the *Good to Great* brands by 3.1 to 1!

Think about that for a second. Marketers love to optimize. But using the traditional techniques for doing so, they can only produce a one to three percent or perhaps in exceptional cases a five to ten percent improvement. Anything over ten percent is worthy of a small office party. What Sisodia, Sheth and Wolfe found—an eightfold increase—is downright remarkable.

What this tells us is simple: in an age of transparency, brands are defined by the totality of their behavior, not their marketing messages. At the core of this behavior is empowerment.

It's not just about empowering consumers (for example, FOEs frequently pay higher employee wages than their counterparts). Instead, the core difference between FOEs and ordinary companies is that they remove friction in their relationships with all of their internal and external partners.

As Sisodia, Sheth and Wolfe proudly note, "If this is not a feel good story, we don't know what is."

Studies about brand behavior have become increasingly popular as companies seek out ways to compete in the modern marketing ecosystem.

One of the largest and most interesting for our purposes was conducted by Siegel & Gale, a global brand and design agency. It ran a six-year study that consisted of a survey completed by over 12,000 consumers in eight countries.

Repeatedly, we saw brands that replace friction with empowerment outperform the competition by orders of magnitude.

In it, consumers were asked to evaluate 585 brands by rating the simplicity and complexity of their products, services, interactions and communications. Analysts then compared these results to industry peers and correlated simplicity to overall financial performance.

In doing so, Siegel & Gale uncovered something profound. A stock portfolio comprising the simplest brands in their Global Top 10 outperformed the average global stock index by 214 percent. That's domination, plain and simple.

The report goes on to state that "the brands that rise to the top of the rankings are those that truly understand what their customers want—and make getting it simple. In addition, simplicity pays for brands that embrace it—garnering greater customer loyalty, fostering innovation among employees and ultimately increasing revenue."

Digging into the numbers, the advantages become even more clear. 69 percent of respondents stated they are more likely to recommend a brand because it provides simpler experiences and communications, and 63 percent said they are willing to pay more for simpler experiences.

As the report concludes, "Consumers live in a world of limitless choices. Brand experience is the road to loyalty. Simplicity will get you there faster."

Our final piece of evidence explains why such simple and empowering brands succeed. Twenty years ago, global management consulting firm Bain & Company found that a 5 percent increase in loyalty often leads to an increase in profit that ranges from 25 to 100%.

By comparison, a 5 percent improvement in any marketing metric—clicks, conversions, laughs from a Super Bowl ad—doesn't do anything remotely close to doubling bottom line profitability. Loyalty matters much more than any other metric, except financials.

Loyalty enables brands to acquire customers at a much lower cost through word-of-mouth marketing. It decreases the need to find new customers because the installed base grows naturally.

It also increases employee retention because job satisfaction increases. But most importantly, it creates a snowball effect because increased profits enable the brand to invest more in customer loyalty.

Bain was not exactly humble about its work. It said its findings were for the business world as "fundamental as the Copernican shift to a sun-centered solar system was for astronomy."

Nonetheless, the study is highly valuable for us, because it shows how critical friction is to the loyalty equation, stating that, "Customers defect at the alarming rate of 10 to 30 percent per year. With this much friction, it is no wonder that productivity and economic growth are languishing. Business is being conducted among strangers, trust is low and energy is sapped."

Nobody in the business world wants to admit it, but despite the trillions of pieces of data available, it's impossible to accurately tie marketing activations to bottom line metrics. Most attempts to do so have been cooked up by those who sell advertising.

The research teams cited here stepped back to look at brand platforms, not marketing activations. Each of the teams used different nomenclature, like "simplicity" and "endearment." They used varied methodologies. Yet, by triangulating the results of their work, we can see a clear pattern emerge: removing friction creates a distinct competitive advantage with a massive and direct impact on financial performance.

4.2

Every new wave of technology creates an existential threat as well as a potential competitive advantage.

Just when brands began to understand desktop computers, mobile became the new challenge. When brands began to understand mobile, social media became the new challenge. When brands began to understand social media, wearables became the new challenge. Screens went from yards to feet to inches away from our faces, carrying an exponentially growing amount of content. Virtual reality is around the corner with technology that almost creates a direct connection to the brain via the optic nerve.

Audiences will become increasingly impatient. Brands will become increasingly transparent. Those that move aggressively will become the next generation's Chobani, Vice Media, Patagonia, Under Armour, Uber or Amazon. Those that fail to do so will be the next generation's Blockbuster, Kodak, MySpace, Borders, Sears, Hummer, BlackBerry or pets.com.

4.3

The power of reciprocity.

The potential of fighting friction through empowerment became clear to me over a few glasses of whiskey with a friend. She had recently married a woman. As we leaned against an upscale brass-and-oak bar, she told me the story of how she came out of the proverbial closet to her family. She was 25 at the time and had grown up in a small Southern town that was not exactly a bastion of liberal ideas and progressive thinking. Her parents were fairly conservative, and she didn't know how it would go.

When brands empower, they turn customers into digitally-enabled brand evangelists.

Thankfully, they were extremely loving and understanding. She told me about warm hugs and happy tears. She revealed how her initial trepidations turned to pure joy, and how she's now closer to her parents than ever before.

But telling the story was still a vulnerable moment for her. She was opening up about one of the most important moments of her life.

As her story progressed, my own need to share a story about a vulnerable moment grew. I was thinking about a specific incident in my own life that demonstrated that everything wasn't always puppies and rainbows in the Rosenblum family. I could almost feel it physically shifting from the back of my mind toward my vocal cords.

Then, she stopped and told me something fascinating. She said that every time she tells this story to someone, that person always feels the need to share something personal in return. It's as if they can't bear the burden of knowing such intimate details without balancing the equation.

At that moment I almost jumped up from the barstool and screamed, "That's it! That's exactly why corporations should try to empower customers." Thankfully I didn't, because it would have ruined the moment and, quite possibly, our friendship.

Maybe I think about brands far more than is healthy, but clearly something was taking place at that bar, and I was determined to figure it out. I eventually learned that it's a psychological phenomenon called reciprocity.

In 1960, Alvin Gouldner wrote the preeminent paper on the topic, which began with a quote from the Roman philosopher Cicero: "There is no duty more indispensable than that of returning kindness...all men distrust one forgetful of a benefit." In other words, people feel obligated to reciprocate.

In a world in which consumers are almost never disconnected from their digital devices, and digital referrals are fundamentally more influential than paid advertising, these obligations are the most powerful form of branding.

Top executives of passion brands seem to understand the power of reciprocity in the most purely positive ways. When I interviewed Kevin Plank, the CEO of Under Armour, for example, he referred to the power of giving "a free gift with purchase." His core philosophy is that Under Armour products should help athletes perform better, not just look better. So he strives to give more value than what his customers pay for.

The value equation becomes out of balance in a good way. Reciprocity motivates their customers to evangelize for the brand, both online and on the ball field.

Human beings want balance. The need for reciprocity coupled with ubiquitous digital connections turn customers into digitally-enabled evangelists who spread the brand message much more effectively than any form of paid media.

4.4

Friction creates a signal.

We've all been there. The sketchy-looking restaurant we've never eaten at before. We don't know the place, and we're not sure if it's OK. But we take a leap of faith and try it out. Then, at some point we go into the bathroom and find that it's gross. It smells bad, there are paper towels on the floor and there's no soap.

Friction creates a signal that affects perceptions long after the moment has passed.

Our first thought isn't about the bathroom. It's about the kitchen. *If that's what they let us see, what does that say about the kitchen behind those closed doors?* Based on a single point of friction, we immediately and permanently create an opinion about the entire business.

These kinds of signals and their implications have been increasingly studied in recent years. Robert Cialdini, a social psychologist frequently referred to as "The Godfather of Influence," offers a good business example of this. A friend of his owned a small jewelry store in Arizona and was having trouble selling a turquoise jewelry collection. It was peak tourist season, and she tried every technique to no avail. Exasperated, she decided to throw in the towel.

When she left town on a buying trip, she wrote a note to her head saleswoman that read, "Everything in this display case, price ½."

When she returned, she was not surprised to find that the jewelry was gone, as lower prices tend to lead to increased demand. What was shocking, however, was that her employee had misread her note and doubled the price instead of cutting it in half. It turned out that shoppers needed a shortcut, and the sky-high price served as a signal for quality. The laws of psychology had trumped the laws of economics.

The implication is clear for brands. Human beings will always take shortcuts. Friction creates a negative signal that affects consumers' perceptions and behavior long after the moment of friction has passed.

Ever-present digital connections have created an almost infinite number of places where brands can interact with consumers. Every single touchpoint in the consumer journey sends critical subconscious signals. As a result, we must fully understand the most granular aspects of that journey and revisit them frequently as technology advances.

Signals and shortcuts reveal how complex and broad the budgeting process needs to be. While incredible advertising campaigns can still build awareness and interest, they can't offset a cascade of negative signals in the consumer journey.

Researchers from Google and the University of Basel in Switzerland studied this exact point and found that users judge a website's aesthetic beauty and perceived functionality in less than .05 seconds, or less time than it takes you to snap your fingers. Based on this initial impression, they decide whether they want to engage or simply click over to the competition.

We can't merely shift dollars away from interruptive messaging. We must also appropriately allocate investments in four major areas: the technology that fuels the consumer experience, the content that provides emotional and rational benefits, the UX design that sends positive signals and the data that seamlessly connects every touchpoint. It's a hell of a lot harder than creating one great brand campaign, but there's absolutely no other choice anymore.

The more evangelists you have,

the fewer ads
you need
to buy.

fi

Antagonist

Advertising can still do amazing things.

But we're asking it to do too much.

Beware of The Machine and The Shiny Objects.

Susie* helped build some of the most successful brands on the planet. Brands that you have in your cupboards right now. She worked for one of the world's largest consumer packaged goods companies.

Our agency was brought in to help it embrace the digital revolution. Not surprisingly, we suggested creating immersive, empowering experiences.

* Name changed for this story

Given that the Mad Men era has been so thoroughly disrupted, why isn't every company fighting friction?

When we shared our ideas, Susie actually laughed at us. Out loud. She then did what she thought was a favor: She broke down the mathematics of how great brands are built. She didn't just talk about how much you should spend on TV vs. print vs. the internet. She also had creative execution down to a science.

She knew exactly how long the ad's main character should be on the screen holding up the product, how long she should smile and then how long the voiceover should spend talking about the product before returning to the star, who would finish the story by sitting comfortably on a couch eating the product and smiling with a friend.

Nothing Susie said was wrong. She was right about the budgeting figures and creative execution. Her recommendations were based on decades of testing and optimization by a team consisting of Harvard graduates, PhDs and other brilliant thinkers.

Her recommendations were based on scientific, optimized truth. Millions upon millions of dollars were invested building her company's model. They knew that if they created a product that hit specific taste scores among a test group, they could apply their proprietary system and create a billion-dollar brand. To her, we were just a bunch of kids with goofy idealistic concepts that weren't tested in the real world.

But Susie's math had a single, devastating flaw. It didn't account for the fact that most people don't sit complacently and watch the entire optimized story anymore. Today, while the protagonist is holding up a product, her audience is checking Instagram. During the voiceover, they are instant messaging. Or worse, they never see the ad in the first place, because they've blocked it or have the sound off.

Given that the Mad Men era has been so thoroughly disrupted, the big mystery is why every company isn't fighting friction.

The Machine refers to the multibillion-dollar industry that drives brands to invest in traditional interruptive advertising.

The answer is The Machine and The Shiny Objects. The Machine refers to the multibillion-dollar industry that drives brands to invest in traditional interruptive advertising. Susie is a cog in the wheel of The Machine.

The Shiny Objects are the bright new tools that distract marketers into thinking they should use the same interruptive tactics while leveraging the newest technologies.

The Machine was originally a great idea. Corporations' use of advertising is one of the key reasons why a small number of countries, America in particular, came to dominate the global economy. It provided a tool to drive capitalism forward by increasing consumer demand. The world's top five economies dominate in the percentage of GDP invested in paid media.

Over time, paid advertising became a massive industry that offered all the data, training and education needed to create world-class brands.

Great careers and trillions of dollars of wealth were built on it. The Machine worked brilliantly for decades.

The top media and advertising technology firms have an entire ecosystem of support: books, blogs, awards, magazines, research firms and conferences all dedicated to the idea that we can build brands through interruptions. An entire town in the south of France gives itself over to the advertising industry every year. In fact, despite the revolutionary change in consumer behavior, growth in paid media continues to outpace the American economy.

The Machine makes it a boatload easier to buy a brand than to build a brand. Marketers can hire an agency to deal with all the headaches of making the creative. Media properties can deal with all the headaches of getting the creative in front of the right eyeballs. And a research company can take away the headaches of measurement and optimization.

Removing friction, by comparison, is extremely difficult. There aren't decades of data to create a template for success, like Susie's TV advertisements. There aren't exact metrics to measure ROI at a granular level.

There isn't a rewards system that provides awards and promotions for empowering customers. But the change is inevitable. The data is clear at a macro level. Consumer behavior is changing at an unprecedented rate. Entire industries are getting disrupted in the blink of an eye. The Machine will continue to churn, but it absolutely must adapt, and do so at a much quicker rate.

This leads us to The Shiny Objects. These are the new, incredible, metric-friendly digital tools: social media, mobile apps, virtual reality, wearable technology. Each of these has been adapted to fit into The Machine's love of interruptions. They are designed to allow for the precise targeting of ads. The technology industry continually creates tools that can impact people's lives in unprecedented ways, and then the marketing industry finds ways to put interruptions into them.

From a macro perspective it makes sense for brands. They've always succeeded by following audiences wherever they go. When women started watching afternoon dramas, Ivory Soap needed to be there, hence the name "soap operas." When social media took off, McDonald's ironically splashed its logo all over the mildly addictive game that enabled users to spend their afternoons building virtual farms.

But just because the audience has shifted to a new media source doesn't mean they want brands to play there in the same interruptive way. There are simply too many brands and too many messages for interruptions to break through.

To study the problem, my firm created a panel of people representing audience segments ranging from teenage girls to middle-aged men. We strapped cameras to their heads and loaded screen-capturing software on their digital devices. We found that they were exposed to a branded message every 2.7 seconds on average. As they consumed social content, they made a decision every 2.1 seconds on average. Without offering some form of value, it's almost impossible for brands to get into the stream and make a meaningful impact.

Yet, The Shiny Objects could be a perfect tool for removing friction. Consumers are almost perpetually connected to a digital device. They look at their mobile device every 6.5 minutes that they are awake. They want brands to play in this ballgame. They want content that informs and empowers. They want to be inspired and educated. They want to make smarter purchase decisions. But they don't want to be interrupted.

TV arrived with a bang after World War II, as a whole new generation was trying to build middle-class lives. Its advent was an amazingly powerful thing. For the first time, sound, pictures and stories came into consumers' living rooms free of charge. Early on, advertising provided a valuable service. It not only provided incredible new content; it also helped educate us about new products and brands. Then Fred Flintstone got in the way.

For its first two years, the show was sponsored by Winston cigarettes. At the end of every show, Fred and Barney would light up Winstons and tell each other how delicious they are, thanks to the filter tip. Fred, Barney and generations of cigarette advertisers made cigarettes seem pretty cool. So people smoked them. Then people got sick. Millions died.

Then, it turned out that the assholes who made those cigarettes knew they were deadly. It didn't take long for the audience to realize that advertising lies. It seems crazy to think that at one point, the audience actually believed advertising. Why wouldn't they? Brands had the trust. Then they broke the trust.

It's not just that the audience avoids ads, it's that they don't even believe them when they see them.

5.3

It's the end of an era.

While conducting research for this book, we interviewed neuroscientists, Ivy League professors and some of the world's top CEOs. We scoured hundreds of consumer interviews and thousands of surveys. We examined white papers, secondary research reports and our own data. But one of the best lessons came while sitting on the couch half-drunk watching cartoons.

It's annoying enough for adults to deal with banner ads and pre-rolls. It will be absolutely unacceptable for the next generation.

Let me explain. My kids are at that wonderful age where if I wake up hungover on a Saturday morning, I get to snuggle with them on the couch and watch cartoons. Thanks to streaming services, we can watch the same cartoons I grew up with.

It's a twisted approach to a basic research method called variable isolation. By watching the same cartoons I watched as a kid, the only real difference is the delivery mechanism.

A few months ago, I put on Netflix, which has all the old DC Comics characters I loved as a kid. We watched my daughter's favorite, Wonder Woman.

Soon, our heroine was battling it out with a bad guy. She found herself in a precarious position, and it looked like she had no escape.

Then the screen went blank. A few seconds later the cartoon came back on. Of course, Wonder Woman escaped her predicament, turned tables on the bad guy and gave him a sound ass-kicking on her way to another superhero victory.

That moment told me everything I need to know about the future of brand building. I was no longer hungover. I was wide awake. I had just witnessed a perfect example of the incredible havoc the digital environment will reap on brands that don't change.

I paused the cartoon and asked my daughter if she had noticed the blank screen. She looked at me like I was from a different planet.

I dug deeper. What just happened? There was a blank screen between the two scenes. Did you see it?

She didn't notice a thing. She just wanted to see Wonder Woman do her thing. I was an annoying interruption.

Again she asked me to put the cartoon back on. Again, I asked her if she noticed what just happened. She had no idea what I was referring to.

Finally, she gave me a look that said *put the fucking cartoon back on, Dad.* So I did. But everything we need to know is in that blank screen that lasted only a second.

The blank screen was a placeholder for a commercial that had originally appeared in the show. My daughter had no idea what it was.

She no longer sees interruptions in the middle of shows. She is being raised with content that either has no ads or has ads that can easily be avoided.

In about ten years, she will have her own discretionary income. Major corporations will want to want to sell her cars, vacations, refrigerators and clothing. But she's not going to wake up and think, *Oh, it's okay, you can interrupt me with your ads now. I grew up without my shows rudely interrupted, but now I'm open to it.*

Kids are now being raised with content on demand. If we use a marketing model based on paid media and interruptions, it will not only be ineffective, it will be counterproductive. It's annoying enough for adults to deal with banner ads and pre-rolls. It will be absolutely unacceptable for the next generation.

5.4

Neuroscience researchers have conducted an experiment dozens of times in which they place a probe into a monkey's brain to measure electrical impulses from their auditory cortex, which produces neural activity when the animal hears sounds.

The researchers then blare a loud, obnoxious sound in the monkey's ear. At first, the monkey's brain goes haywire. The probe shows an enormous amount of activity in the monkey's brain. This is not surprising.

Then, they repeat the loud, obnoxious sound. Again, the probe shows an enormous amount of activity in the monkey's brain. Again, this is not surprising. Nor is it surprising when it happens when they repeat the process a few more times.

What is incredibly surprising, however, is that the reaction doesn't last. After a small handful of exposures, the monkey's brain stops reacting. In a graph, the amplitude of neural activity for the repeated sounds looks like the side of a cliff.

The monkey has an internal defense mechanism. It normalizes its brain activity. It ignores the blaring obnoxious sound. The physiological phenomenon is called repetition suppression. The monkey's brain suppresses the barrage of sounds. It can't continue to dramatically respond because it would be incapable of managing its other responsibilities, such as eating, sleeping, socializing and fornicating.

Consumers are just like those monkeys. We see a branded message almost every second we are awake. On average, we see 5,000 per day. That's more than double the previous generation. Thanks to the proliferation of media and targeting technology, the paid media industry continues to grow over 5 percent annually.

But those messages have become largely ignored. Like monkeys, humans also have a self-defense mechanism. They normalize and disregard the constant barrage. Repetition suppression is a survival mechanism, and it's more powerful than paid media.

5.5

Fighting friction is not a new phenomenon.

Branding was always difficult and only briefly became easy. As the 1800s gave way to the 1900s, people talked about concepts that were similar to friction. They had just lived through an era in which big capitalists had treated them horribly, and they voted people like Teddy Roosevelt into power to clean house. Across the country, journalists like Upton Sinclair exposed horrific practices, and the government took action.

Prior to TV, brands needed to empower if they wanted to impress.

The entirety of industry had a friction problem, one that was serious enough that it led to the establishment of communism in many countries. That didn't happen in Great Britain, however. A modest amount of the credit goes to Cadbury.

At the time, workers at many companies were organizing strikes, and the owners were using thugs to try to break them. But the leaders of Cadbury, George and Richard Cadbury, were devout Quakers. Being pacifists, beating the hell out of reluctant workers was off the table for them. Instead, they decided to attack the friction of the business world itself. In 1879, they began paying their workers a generous living wage and dabbling in pensions. But that was only the beginning.

They also hated the crowded, urban conditions in which Industrial Age workers were forced to live. So in 1893 they bought a large, rural parcel of land and developed a model town, Bourneville. Forget buying a few ads to build their brand. They hired an architect and built an entire community. The workers' cottages were spacious, with modern designs and their own gardens. Cadbury then added swimming facilities, a clubhouse, a grass running track, soccer fields, fishing ponds, walking paths and so on.

Not only did the company want its workers to be comfortable, it wanted them to live healthy, active lives (the only downside was that, being Quakers, they didn't allow a pub). Even today, the lovely little town consistently ranks as one of the most livable in the country.

Cadbury, of course, was a huge success. Not only were its workers fiercely loyal and highly productive, but the brand also reaped a massive harvest of positive PR. The same muckraking journalists who savaged the meat industry fawned over Cadbury. It was held up as a model of how capitalism could work in a way that benefited everyone. Macro friction was removed, and the model was repeated across Great Britain by dozens of other companies.

Fighting friction is not new. Prior to the arrival of TV, brands needed to empower if they wanted to impress. It was only for a brief period of time—60 years or so—that no one cared about friction and empowerment, and sought instead to entertain and obfuscate.

This brief period was a wonderful time for brands. The audience was complacent and attentive. For the first time in history, brands could be both lazy and effective. They could hire a handsome pitchman to sell people the latest and great products. Millions watched, believed and purchased.

Brands were built this way. Great brands. Ones we all know. Sadly for many, those days are over.

It's easy to call this insane, but the simple fact is that it's institutionalized muscle memory.

Marketers keep doing the same thing because that's what they know how to do.

si

Alignment

Alignment is the ultimate friction fighter.

Brands also have a hierarchy of needs.

The psychologist Abraham Maslow, when he was trying to understand human nature, came up with his famed hierarchy of needs. Like everything in academia, it has been argued, modified and footnoted to death, but like most good ideas, it has also endured. Maslow envisioned human beings as having a pyramid of needs. At the bottom of the pyramid you find basic needs, like food, water and shelter. Next come safety and security, then love and belonging, and finally at the top you find self-actualization, or being the person you want to be.

In Maslow's vision, in order to move up a level, each of the needs below it has to be fulfilled. If you're scraping by on a bowl of rice a day, you're going to focus on your empty stomach, not your inner happiness. As soon as you have enough to eat, you can attend to your safety and security. Once you're safe, you graduate to belonging and love, and so on. Self-actualization isn't important if you are starving to death.

Brands also have a hierarchy of needs, but most have built their hierarchy upside down. Based on overall expenditures, interruptive advertising typically occupies the widest, most foundational part of the pyramid.

Sure, every company talks about serving the customer, and most talk about creating valuable content. But, the truth is that for many companies, over 80 percent of marketing budgets still goes to paid media. Once they've gotten that out of the way, whatever is left goes to web development, usability testing and content creation.

A single 30-second TV advertisement on a top TV show costs about half a million dollars, not including creative development fees. Brands buy ads by the bucketful, but very few people see or care about them. By contrast, user-friendly experiences are cheap, and everybody cares about that.

The foundation of the pyramid should not be paid advertising. At the foundation should be leadership, which is simply about getting an entire organization aligned for a specific goal.

From there, it's about empowering the audience through content that improves category performance and experiences that improve the brand relationship. With that foundation in place, advertising can be effectively and efficiently used as the final stage of the hierarchy.

On the following pages are the four key stages of the brand hierarchy: Frictionless Leadership, Frictionless Categories, Frictionless Commerce and Frictionless Advertising. The first two stages can be skipped and still create a good brand. There's no shame in that. But a brand that wants to create passionate, emotional relationships with its customers must follow each of these key stages in order.

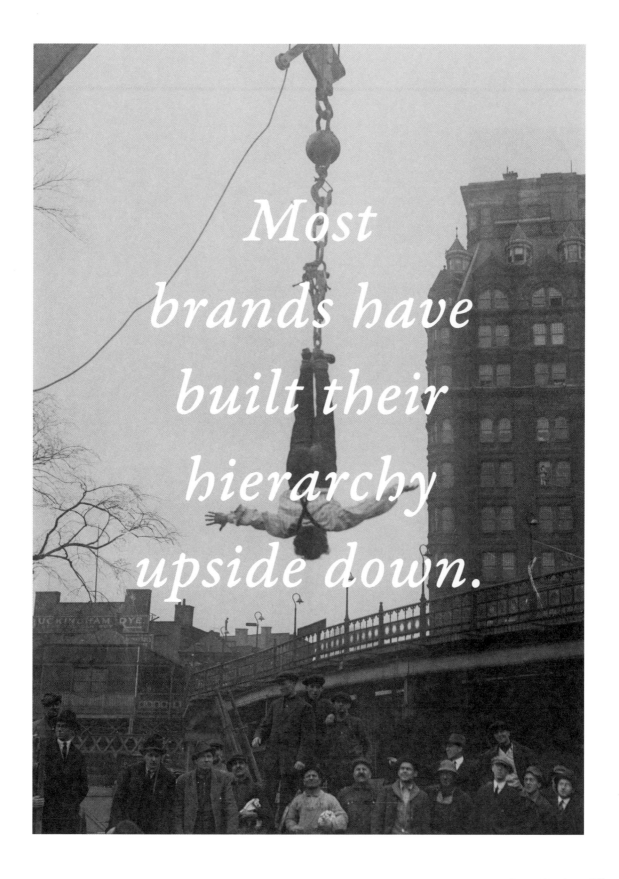

Most brands have built their hierarchy upside down.

Frictionless Leadership

Strong leadership removes internal friction by ensuring a team is aligned on a common goal. It permeates every aspect of the organization.

Winning brands stand for something bigger than a great product and more meaningful than entertaining advertisements. It all starts with leadership. Time and again, we find that brands that empower consumers have strong leadership. Leadership with conviction. Leadership with a purpose. Leadership that is clear, concise and compelling.

Strong leadership removes internal friction by ensuring a team is aligned on a common goal. It permeates every aspect of the organization, including finance, staffing, internal communication and external marketing activations. It provides a reason for being in business and a purpose for every investment.

It helps organizations maximize their return on investment for every resource because it prevents the waste of unfocused experimentation. It ensures all actions create synergies.

To be clear, it's not about charismatic leadership. Research shows that extroverts and introverts perform similarly from a bottom-line success standpoint. Rather, it's about having a clear viewpoint about what is right for the internal team, for business partners and for consumers. It's about investing in a communication cadence that maintains an unwavering focus on the organization's purpose and the exact behaviors required to reach that purpose.

Frictionless Categories

Effective content has a point of view. It stretches the imagination and pushes the audience to think and feel differently than ever before.

Creating Frictionless Categories is the exciting part of marketing, where you find the cool case studies mentioned throughout this book. It's about creating content and tools that help people achieve their personal dreams. Effective content stretches the imagination and pushes the audience to think and feel differently than ever before.

Consumers have an insatiable need for content. Brands are in a perfect position to provide this content for the simple reason they can focus on thinly sliced audiences. They can let CNN and ESPN provide content for the masses. In fact, great content won't resonate with an entire customer base. It's about finding a small, influential segment of consumers who are ready to fully emotionally engage with the brand.

A recent study demonstrated that customers that are committed at a deep emotional level are 52 percent more valuable, on average, than those who are just highly satisfied. It's content that creates this shift to deep emotional engagement. Great products can only make customers highly satisfied.

It's important to recognize that it's not just about one-way content creation. Consumers don't merely want to hear a brand story. They want to help create the story. They want to turn life into their own authentic adventure, and they want to share what they learn. Frictionless categories not only empower people to have better experiences. They empower people to participate in the conversation.

Frictionless Commerce

Ironically, every technological innovation that makes it easier for consumers to buy products makes it more difficult for brands to sell products.

Frictionless commerce is about removing the micro friction that makes it difficult for customers to make educated purchases or fully leverage the products they already own.

Ironically, every technological innovation that makes it easier for consumers to buy products makes it more difficult for brands to sell products. Screens are getting both smaller, in the form of wearable technology, and bigger in the form of smart TVs. Many screens are being replaced altogether with voice-activated technology.

It's not just that consumers expect brands to make products available in these new environments. They want extensive, transparent, personalized information that is seamlessly connected across their devices.

No amount of effective branding can overcome usability flaws. This creates an expensive mind shift for brands, because it requires a focus on technology, data and user experience, not broad-based messaging. It's more difficult, dynamic and expensive than it sounds.

Given the explosive growth of start-ups that remove friction from the entire brand relationship, the bar is continually being raised. Consumers expect usability to be crystal clear on the dozens of touchpoints that attempt to shift them from a prospect to a customer to a brand evangelist.

Frictionless Advertising

This isn't about the death of advertising. That false eulogy has been written before.

Advertising is vital, but it's been living in the wrong part of the hierarchy for too long. Jeff Bezos, founder of Amazon, summarized this perfectly: "I'm not saying that advertising is going away. But the balance is shifting. If today the successful recipe is to put 70 percent of your energy into shouting about your service and 30 percent into making it great, over the next 20 years I think that's going to invert."

Making advertising the last chronological stage of investment creates a frictionless environment where ads are no longer asked to carry the entire message. They just need to be a gateway to empowering experiences. The entire brand story does not need to be included in an interruptive, abbreviated message.

Additionally, frictionless advertising lives in a virtuous cycle of improved targeting and enhanced content. When users interact with content, they provide very specific data about their demographics, psychographics and needs for emotional and rational content.

This data can then be used to improve the targeting and messaging of subsequent ads. As users interact with those ads, they provide additional demographic, psychographic and behavioral data that can then be used to optimize content.

This virtuous cycle is fueled by data, creates data and is improved by data. Over time, it makes the advertising more streamlined and targeted while making the content more immersive and valuable.

Want to create a great ad? An ad that makes people laugh out loud? An ad that carries your brand message in an authentic and meaningful way? An ad that goes beyond winning awards and actually increases market share?

The action item is a bit counterintuitive: to create a great ad, focus less on advertising. Spend less time, less money, less energy and less resources on creative. First focus inward on your own behavior. Create a great brand platform that empowers your audience. One that educates, enriches and inspires. After you've done that, you can create a world-class ad because it will simply need to put a creative lens on the experience.

Advertising no longer needs to tell the entire brand story. It is simply a key piece of a connected experience, not just from a messaging standpoint, but also from a data standpoint. Every interaction with both advertisements and immersive content creates behavioral data, which feeds a virtuous cycle for optimizing ad targeting, audience traffic generation and content creation.

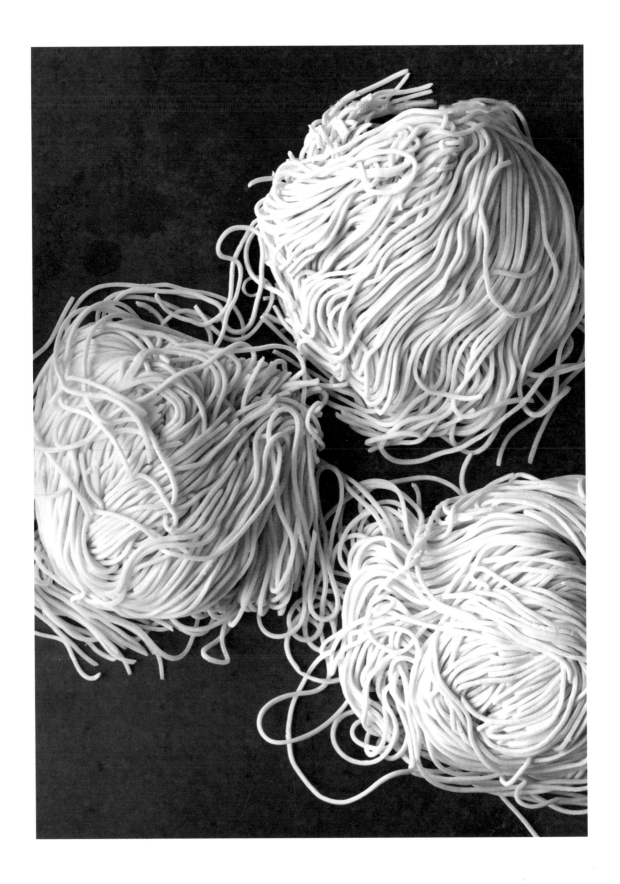

The three keys to frictionless organizations.

Before he was a James Beard Award–winning chef, before he received Michelin stars, before he won chef of the year, before he was recognized as one of the world's 100 most influential people, before he became a magazine publisher, TV personality and international star, David Chang was just a dude who didn't want to wear a suit to work every day.

After attending a prestigious prep school and college, he went to the French Culinary Institute. When he graduated, he got a job at one of New York City's best restaurants, Craft, working for one of the world's top chefs, Tom Colicchio.

He worked in a kitchen full of all-stars, most of whom went on to become critically acclaimed themselves. But cooking incredible, artistic meals wasn't what David wanted to do. He wanted to serve noodles. Ramen noodles, to be precise. An upscale version of the crappy ramen noodles you ate in college.

So he left his incredible job and headed to Japan on a vision quest to learn how the best noodles are made. His father's friend set him up with an apprenticeship at a small restaurant in Tokyo. He had visions of learning from the word's best. He knew it would be demanding work, learning from a life master. But he was willing to spend hours toiling in the bowels of the finest establishment, learning the craft.

Unfortunately, that's not what he found waiting for him in Japan. Instead, he found a man who lived and cooked in tighty-whiteys—stretched out, sagging tighty-whiteys with a newspaper tucked into the waistband. The newspaper served as a kitchen towel. A cigarette hung from his mouth at all times. His skin was gray, and he was constantly surrounded by a cloud of smoke. He left meat festering on the warm counter.

Despite his intentions, David only lasted a few days. He was ready to return home, hat in hand. Then his father's friend found another opportunity for him. This one was the polar opposite of the first.

David began working with the samurai master of udon noodles, Akio Hosoda. The man and his wife ran a restaurant on the first floor of their two-story home. The couple served only 15 meals a day.

They weren't in it for the money. Their goal was to craft the finest noodles that were humanly possible. They ground the flour by hand every day. They spent hours kneading, stretching and cutting the noodles to absolute perfection.

David spent weeks learning the dough mixing technique, but was not allowed to use it for a single noodle served to customers. When it was time to learn cutting, Akio only allowed him to cut newspaper at first.

After months of dedication, David finally earned his mentor's respect. He was allowed to make noodles and cook the dishes. They started to bond as master and apprentice. David's vision quest was being fulfilled.

Until one of David's friends came to visit. While enjoying the noodles and cold Japanese beer, he let slip to Akio that David's true passion was ramen noodles, not udon.

This is a small difference for you and me. It's the world to an udon master. David explained in his book, *Momofuku*, "To Akio, the idea that I was at his restaurant dithering in soba when my real goals were tied to a completely different noodle was tantamount to treason."

It was curtains for David. There was only one path for Akio. It's either udon or nothing. One moment, David was creating a lifetime of memories. The next moment, he was ceremoniously given a rolling pin and asked to leave. If he wasn't committed to what Akio deeply believed in, he was out.

Only one percent of leaders excel at all three elements required for success.

As I heard this *Kung Fu Panda*–esque story, it stuck with me because Akio had found his own path to what I affectionately refer to as the "$20 billion research study," which reveals the three keys to frictionless leadership.

The research was conducted by a consulting firm founded by Geoff Smart. Known as ghSMART, the company strives to "help leaders amplify their positive impact on the world." I refer to it as the $20 billion research study because they interviewed 20 self-made billionaires about the core principles of successful leadership.

These interviews were actually just a small component of the research. They also conducted 15,000 interviews with business leaders, military generals, head surgeons and school principals. The list included more than 30 CEOs of multibillion-dollar companies. In total, they compiled more than 9 million data points and worked with the University of Chicago to independently analyze the data.

In the end, they found that leadership success really boils down to three areas, which they call a Power Score. It's a sort-of acronym of "priorities, who and relationships."

According to Geoff's data, leaders who nail all three areas—prioritizing, hiring and building team relationships—dominate the competition. Those in the top 10 percent are twice as likely as average to succeed, and 20 times as likely as those in the bottom 10 percent.

Of course, it's not easy to do these things. Most leaders are best at relationships, with a 46 percent success rate. Only 24 percent succeed at prioritizing, and a dismal 14 percent can hire well. Only one percent of leaders excel at all three elements.

The critical ingredient is a commitment to the result: a mission that is authentic, inspiring, realistic and can be supported with everyday behaviors.

Let's pause to think about that for a moment. They have 9 million data points that can be easily organized into three commonsense categories, yet 99 out of 100 leaders are unsuccessful at doing all of them. Talk about upside potential.

As I went around the country speaking to C-level executives from industry-leading brands for this book, it was amazing to see how closely their philosophies and actions mirrored the study's findings. Over and over again, successful leaders build systems that are so elegantly simple that it became frustrating to listen to them. The keys to success are both obvious and rarely followed in totality.

The first part of the equation is priorities, but in order to prioritize, you need to know why you're prioritizing in the first place. That starts with a clear and compelling mission.

Most companies do not have strong, clear, differentiated mission statements. In *Winning*, Jack Welch described typical mission statements as "generic platitudes that do nothing but leave employees directionless or cynical." In contrast, he noted that, "A good mission statement and a good set of values are so real they smack you in the face with their concreteness. The mission announces exactly where you are going, and the values describe the behaviors that will get you there."

Returning to Yvon Chouinard and the Patagonia example, their mission statement is to, "Build the best product, cause no unnecessary harm, use business to inspire and implement solutions to the environmental crisis."

Most organizations feel stretched thin, which is a side effect of insufficient focus.

Of course, Patagonia isn't some nonprofit, hippie endeavor. It is one of the most successful brands on the planet. Yvon and his team make it abundantly clear that they are about profit and growth. They don't simply want to have a big company. They also want to influence the behavior of other companies.

They hammer on their core theme relentlessly. It's not simply about a message. It is almost impossible to interact with Patagonia in any way where they are not overtly defending the environment. That's a massive shift away from typical corporate messaging, and it could easily create friction. But, their clear mission aligns their behavior at every turn, beginning with the team they've hired.

Nobody works at Patagonia because they simply want a cool job making cool outdoor gear. They want to be part of a movement, one with a higher calling that attracts like-minded individuals. That's what frictionless leadership does. Everyone knows exactly why they are there and what they want to accomplish.

To understand the concept more fully, let's look at a company enjoying success with the same formula in a completely different category.

Seventh Generation is a personal care and cleaning brand. Based in Burlington, Vermont, its team members don't consider themselves a business with a mission. They proudly state that "Seventh Generation is a mission-driven business." And that mission is clear: "To inspire a consumer revolution that nurtures the health of the next seven generations."

That's very far from drab corporate speak about shareholder value. It's a rallying cry that drives people to create something more than just a product. It serves as a challenge to the entire team and affects everything they do and every decision they make.

Recently, they gathered the entire team for a full day dedicated to focusing on the mission, with a series of discussions and exercises created to reinforce their mission and communicate exactly what it means to all aspects of the business.

Most organizations that I speak to feel stretched thin, which is a side effect of insufficient focus. Seventh Generation, on the other hand, paused for a full day to simply reflect upon their mission.

More importantly, they use it as a touchstone in every meeting so they start all discussions focused in on what they should be doing. Every tactical decision must ladder up to their strategic goal of inspiring a consumer revolution that nurtures multiple generations.

Just as Akio was not going to tolerate someone who did not put udon above all else, they are ardent about rejecting ideas that don't support their mission. As Joey Bergstein, their CMO and General Manager, told me, "Just because you can, doesn't mean you should."

There is no proven formula for creating an effective mission. The critical ingredient is a commitment to the result: a mission that is authentic, inspiring, realistic and can be supported with everyday behaviors.

For example, when the Navy Seals needed a credo, they flew a bunch of their people out to San Clemente Island with a couple of cases of beer, firewood and some raw meat, and said, "Have at it." The resulting credo can easily be found online. It is so unique, compelling and distinctly Navy Seals that it will send shivers down your spine.

With the mission statement in place, an organization can move on to fulfilling the mission with an established set of priorities. The reason most leaders fail at this is not that they don't have priorities. Rather, they create too many that don't ladder up to the mission.

In fact, ghSMART's data reveals that 90 percent of leaders who have low scores in prioritization tend to pursue an excessive number of priorities. That is probably because leaders tend to be entrepreneurial and optimistic by nature. They see opportunities that many would miss. Being optimistic is a positive attribute, in general, but it can also lead to activities that distract from the core mission.

A clear and limited set of priorities allows you to concentrate on what matters: building synergies and driving sustainable success. It keeps teams focused. If you have one or two things that don't ladder back to the core mission, you can quickly get derailed and soon find yourself playing defense rather than offense. The key to successful prioritization is documenting, communicating and adhering to the priorities. It's a process, not an event.

With priorities in place, the next part of the equation is building the team to meet those priorities. According to the ghSMART data, one bad hire costs a company 15 times the base salary of the employee, on average. Meaning, a bad hire with a $100,000 annual salary costs a company $1.5 million.

That's pretty scary. But here's where it gets outright alarming: 50 percent of hires are unsuccessful, according to their data. Given that only 14 percent of leaders are great at hiring, this should be the top opportunity for almost all organizations.

Success starts with a clear definition of an A player, which is "a candidate who has at least a 90 percent chance of achieving a set of outcomes that only the top 10 percent of possible candidates could achieve."

Given the upside potential of hiring A players, it's not surprising to find that companies that have disrupted entire industries are taking revolutionary approaches to building their teams. Airbnb, for example, applied journey mapping to the recruiting process. They held internal brainstorming sessions to map out the ideal experience, remove any sources of friction and understand the key emotions associated with each stage of a candidate's path to employment. Then, they created content and tools to move qualified candidates along their journey.

The tactics used by Airbnb are not groundbreaking when looked at individually. For example, they send emails to candidates that outline key steps and provide background information, including culture videos, FAQs and other information. Yet, each step both moves the candidate along the journey and sends positive signals about employment at Airbnb.

A great hiring process is core to fighting friction.

Hiring A players starts with a clear scorecard that establishes a strong mission for each prospective employee.

It's actually very similar to how they interact with their customers. They remove small pieces of friction at every juncture, which builds positive momentum toward conversion and evangelism.

Ideo is another cutting-edge business that created a unique approach to hiring A players. It is one of the world's most successful design companies. Its managers found that success at their firm depends on what they call T-shaped people. The vertical bar in the T represents a deep level of expertise in a specific area, and the horizontal bar represents a broad array of interests that leads to strong collaboration with team members from varying disciplines.

Since Ideo routinely designs products that revolutionize industries, brainstorming is a critical component of their process and success. T-shaped people naturally hear other people's ideas and build on them.

This requires two personality traits: empathy, which enables them to look at a challenge from another perspective, and enthusiasm, which helps them add energy and build on ideas.

Simply being an expert in one area, an I shape, doesn't build synergies with experts from other disciplines. Teams built with I-shaped people can develop good ideas, but it's much harder for them to create revolutionary ideas.

As a result, Ideo managers have turned conversations with prospective hires into an art form. They've learned to look for specific cues that can't be covered on a resume. For example, T-shaped people naturally gravitate toward discussing aspects of collaboration and the success of others around them.

They tend not to focus on what they have accomplished themselves, but rather talk about others who inspire them.

Just as Airbnb put a tremendous effort into its hiring process, Ideo commits massive resources toward finding T-shaped people. They create content about their process that naturally appeals to the right candidates and explains exactly what they're looking for. This transparency serves as a magnet—and helps pare down the list of applicants.

Whether it's Airbnb using a journey map or Ideo looking for T-shaped people, successful team building is about defining the exact type of person you need to meet your organization's priorities, documenting those traits and then building a process to recruit people who have them.

So how do you separate the people you need from those you don't? ghSMART suggests that it starts with a clear scorecard that establishes a strong mission for each prospective employee. You then define five to seven outcomes that show what successful performance looks like, as well as the core capabilities that are critical to achieve those outcomes.

It's a simple step that's rarely taken. We document everything in the business world, but we don't document the exact mission, skills and, perhaps most importantly, personality traits we're looking for in a candidate. But recruiting without a clear scorecard is like running a business without a documented business plan.

With an effective scorecard in place, the interviewing process comes down to methodically and exhaustively ascertaining whether a candidate has the required character and skills for success. Effective interviewing is not about "getting to know" the candidate; it's about leveraging techniques similar to investigative journalism. In each interview, the goal is to drive toward specific experiences and behaviors that match with the mission and priorities outlined in the scorecard.

Hypothetical questions such as "what would you do in this situation?" are a common malady. Industrial psychology proves they don't work. Effective interviewing is about digging deeper and deeper into specific actions and decisions made during the candidate's career, with an emphasis on finding repeated patterns.

This is often difficult because relentlessly digging is an uncomfortable process for both participants. It often requires over 10 hours of interviews for each successful candidate, using a team approach with each interviewer assigned to specific questions, rather than creating redundancies that ultimately teach the candidate what the organization is looking for.

Success is based on effective cross-disciplinary communication. Silos kill.

The final part of the leadership equation—relationships—may sound touchy-feely. It's not. To create amazing work, you need the whole to be greater than the sum of its parts. Every facet of an organization must work together, including retail, customer service, technology, product development, operations, legal and finance. That requires relationships that are based on effective cross-disciplinary communication. Silos kill.

Kevin Plank seems to have been born to do this. Before he was the founder and CEO of Under Amour, he was the special teams captain on the University of Maryland football team. The leader of the special teams isn't typically the biggest, fastest or best athlete. Instead, he has to be a fearless leader. A person who is willing to do whatever it takes to make the play and motivate his teammates.

Plank used this same competitive DNA to start Under Armour in his grandmother's basement and then grow it into one of the world's most successful brands. Under Armour's mission is to "make all athletes better through passion, design and the relentless pursuit of innovation."

Kevin builds Under Armour's competitive culture in a relatively simple way: he treats his organization like a sports team, and he is clearly the head coach. Perhaps his most important coaching technique is leveraging the white boards that he keeps in his office, which he uses to relentlessly hammer on his key priorities.

The white board is three panels across and five panels deep. He notes, "On one, I keep sayings or slogans—dictate the tempo, listen more than you talk—and at the center of my whiteboards sits our pillars of greatness as we call them:

Make great product, tell a great story, service our business and, most importantly, build a great team of people." He uses the board to ensure that he and his team never waver from their core beliefs or priorities.

A few minutes with Kevin makes you want to jump out of your seat and compete because he hammers on their relentless pursuit of innovation to help athletes perform better. It's clear. It's concise. It's differentiating. He uses a simple yet authentic technique to repeat his priorities. He leads his leaders. He ensures they are focused on the mantras and the priorities necessary to meet their mission.

The white board might seem fairly trivial, but it's paramount because it's emblematic of something bigger. Kevin proves that leadership is about conviction and cadence. The white board is simply a foundational tool that ensures that every behavior by the company is aligned. They do no vacillate.

Of course, not all leaders should emulate Kevin Plank in every detail. Most are not former special teams captains, and it would be inauthentic to behave like a football coach if that's not in your organization's DNA.

For a different approach, let's look at Chris Crayner, the Chief Digital Officer at Universal Orlando Resorts. His team's mission is to relentlessly pursue data to ensure that guests have the best possible vacation. He uses a customer centricity model. As he explains, "It's a movement away from a campaign model to an interaction model. It shifts the focus from one-to-many to one-to-one." His core belief is that, "Every interaction drops a data trail. The real magic is in following the context."

To get his team to understand this, he has an analogy he calls the starry field. He asks them to close their eyes and imagine themselves on a hill on a cloudless night. They can look up and see a billion stars twinkling above them. Now, he asks them to imagine that every twinkling light is a customer engaging with Universal in some way. They're calling, clicking on a search term or going into a resort.

Then he asks his team, "Are you responding to that signal with every piece of institutional knowledge and data you have to make that interaction as relevant and valuable as possible?"

To fulfill the vision, Chris created a system he calls a customer relationship factory, which enables his team to act on the relevant moments in the starry field. A centerpiece of the factory is a guest journey map that they turned sideways so they can focus on the data inputs and outputs.

The goal of the map is to determine the right content that advances prospects and customers at every interaction point along the journey from prospect to evangelist. This enables them to focus on the needs of the guest rather than the needs of the internal teams.

The factory uses an approach based on agile software development, which includes a documented process for integrating cross-departmental teams for rapid iteration. Core to the cadence is a daily standing scrum for managing daily sprints, and quarterly meetings where team members are held accountable for meeting specific plans for empowering guests through an interaction model.

This regular, repeating communication cadence keeps cross-departmental teams aligned and allows them to act on the starry field analogy through a series of brief, repeatable, optimized sprints. It ensures that each team member is not only meeting the day-to-day requirements for success, but also advancing the overarching vision and capabilities.

What both Chris Crayner and Kevin Plank demonstrate is that successful business relationships are about conviction and cadence. It's about having clear priorities and straightforward, repeatable tools to maintain focus on them.

Kevin Plank happily plays the role of coach, urging his team forward with motivational catch phrases and a laser focus on key priorities. Chris Crayner repeats the starry field analogy and uses agile development principles to act on it. The methods are quite different, but they're both authentic. They have an unwavering focus on a core message and a cadence to communicate that message. They're not shy about repetition. Rather, they embrace it a key tenet of success.

While the aforementioned leaders are running organizations that generate billions of dollars in revenue, the underlying principles are no different from those of Aiko, the humble noodle master in Japan. He wants to make the best possible udon he can possibly create, and every behavior ladders back to that simple goal. He had one of the world's greatest culinary talents under his wing, but because that talent did not share his vision, they parted ways.

Perhaps it was Aiko's influence, but a zen-like thought came to mind again while interviewing business leaders for the book: There are no failures when organizations are aligned.

Even unsuccessful tactics create institutional knowledge toward a larger goal. Unlike teams that treat strategy like a process of trial and error, alignment shifts risk from the strategic level to the tactical level. When there is full alignment through frictionless leadership, even small missteps are part of the path to success.

6.4

90 percent of the world's data was collected in the past two years

Every day, we create 2.5 quintillion bytes of data. Every click, every tap and every purchase we make are tracked. But that's just the beginning. Mobile technology tracks our exact location. Wearable technology tracks our behavior. Neuroscience tracks our thought patterns.

Capturing data is table stakes. Every brand has data. Data is going to come from everywhere, right down to our pillows. The amount of data available and its implications on personal privacy are scary. But there's also unprecedented utility that can be provided.

Passion brands will be built by those that are internally structured to capitalize on the data.

Fighting friction starts with pointing intellectual and creative firepower **inward** at behavior

before pointing it outward with messaging.

sev

Irony

You can't fight friction externally until you remove friction internally.

7.1

Feed your creativity.

Phineas Gage was a strong, intelligent and energetic man. A natural leader, he rose quickly through the ranks of construction crews and by his mid-20s was the head of a team that built roadbeds in Vermont.

One September afternoon in 1848, Phineas bored a deep hole in a rock. He filled it with explosives and was packing the top with sand using an eight-foot-long tamping iron. He got distracted for a moment, and the iron sparked against the rock. The powder exploded. The tamping iron was propelled from the hole and into the left side of Phineas's face. It passed behind his left eye and exited out the top of his skull, flying with such force that it landed point-first like a javelin 80 feet away. It was covered with Phineas's brains and blood.

Amazingly enough, Phineas did not die. In fact, he was conscious and alert when his crew brought him out of the hills into town. When a doctor came to examine him, he was sitting in front of his hotel, greeting friends and telling them the tale. The doctor didn't believe the story until Phineas vomited about a half a teacupful of brain onto the floor.

Digital technology has wreaked havoc on our brains.

Phineas lost another ounce of his brain during surgery, but he fought through and eventually recovered. Soon after, however, his friends and family noticed he wasn't the same man. His intelligence and memory remained intact, but his affable personality had changed. He became impatient, short-fused and aggressive. He went from a leader of men to virtually unemployable. The rod had not only scarred his face; it had fundamentally altered his personality.

Phineas's case turned out to be a seminal moment for the scientific community. It helped them realize that the human brain has different regions that perform specific functions. His intellect remained intact after his injury, but very specific personality traits were altered. A century and a half later, the findings from this gruesome incident have never had stronger implications.

Like Phineas's tamping iron, digital technology has wreaked havoc on our brains. The great irony is that the same innovations that have produced a revolutionary business environment also severely impact our ability to be creative in it.

The simple truth is that great brands are built by creative people. With all the new digital technology, we need creative people more than ever. The world is changing at an exponential rate. Every brand has limitless access to data and technology. Creativity creates the true competitive advantage.

To understand why, let's step back to see how the human brain works. It developed over millions of years. Evolutionarily speaking, a cross section of the brain is similar to a cross section of a tree. The oldest parts are in the middle, and the newer developments are on the outside.

Most important to our discussion is the amygdala, which is found just about dead-center in your skull. It's part of the limbic system and helps manage our emotions. In particular, it controls the fight-or-flight response, a series of physiological changes that occur whenever you encounter stress.

If you're attacked by a woolly mammoth, for example, blood immediately rushes to your vital organs and away from your extremities.

We need to feed our creativity, while avoiding needless digital attacks on our brains. It's more difficult than it sounds.

Your fingertips and toes become cold, because they're less important than your liver. You're not hungry. You're not horny. You're not creative. You're just trying to survive.

The amygdala manages the secretion of two fight-or-flight response hormones, adrenaline and cortisol. It doesn't take the sudden appearance of a wooly mammoth to trigger their release. Your mobile device is more than enough. That weird feeling you get in your gut when your phone buzzes is your amygdala leaping into action.

This happens because the vast majority of the information we get on our devices is a threat at a physiological level. Because humans have something called a negativity bias, we react more strongly to negative than positive experiences.

This was a powerful tool when we had to avoid woolly mammoths. Now, we generally don't need to worry about getting eaten, but it remains with us. The negativity bias is why, for example, the nightly news is filled with horrible stories. Newsmakers know that bad news drives up viewership.

When it comes to digital interruptions, we naturally seek out and are affected more powerfully by bad stuff. So your phone delivers you Amber Alerts and warnings about traffic. Work email is particularly bad, because it frequently contains an urgent problem.

This has a profound effect on our creativity. Adrenaline and cortisol don't merely shut down blood flow to our extremities. They reduce the performance of key areas of our brain, including the prefrontal cortex. This is one of the most recent and advanced areas of the brain, and it is critical for creative thinking and the formation of memories. The problem is that the amygdala can be hijacked with stress. When it is, it takes over our prefrontal cortex. It kills our creativity.

It's not just that mobile devices impact our day-to-day creative thinking. They also prevent creative breakthroughs. This was demonstrated by Mark Beeman, a neuroscientist and former Olympic hopeful who turned his competitive energy toward isolating the "eureka" part of the brain.

It's not just that mobile devices impact our creative thinking. They also prevent creative breakthroughs.

He was an expert in fMRI technology, which measures blood flow in the brain. This roughly indicates the areas of the brain that are activated during specific tasks. He teamed up with John Kounios, a specialist in EEG technology, which measures electrical activity in the brain. Together they realized that EEG could provide a readout on timing while fMRI showed which region of the brain was active during breakthrough creative moments.

To do so, they gave subjects a series of complex word puzzles and then monitored their brains as they attempted to solve them. Through this process, they discovered a specific region of the brain, called the anterior superior temporal gyrus (aSTG). It is a small region that sits on the right hemisphere just above the ear. The experiments showed that about 30 milliseconds before a subject solved a puzzle, an electrical surge would occur in the aSTG.

Finding this region of the brain was a remarkable accomplishment. More importantly, Beeman and Kounios were able to watch the brain's process prior to

when it activated the aSTG. It turned out that it ignited only after the brain scanned through many different regions looking for the answer to the puzzle, particularly in the left hemisphere. It was only when the brain searched every key region and was fully stumped that the aSTG was activated. That's when the epiphany occurred.

Here's the problem for those of us trying to develop friction-fighting breakthrough ideas: When we turn to Facebook, Google, Siri, Instagram or any of the other seemingly infinite digital tools every few minutes that we are awake, we don't give our brains enough time to get fully stumped. We don't activate our aSTG. Our digital connections prevent the eureka moment.

So how do we fix all this? Creative health, it turns out, is a lot like physical health. If you have a heart attack, your doctor isn't going to simply say cut back on carbs. She'll create a holistic program that involves diet, exercise and stress reduction.

By the time you're done reading this paragraph, another 14 books about mindfulness will have been published. But this isn't a book about yoga, meditation or the power of kale. You already know that you need to sleep more, meditate more and eat more fiber. This is a book about growing great brands.

As with many problems, the first step is admitting you have one. Our problem is addiction. We are addicted to adrenaline and cortisol. You might wonder how we can be addicted to something so fundamentally unpleasant. People are usually addicted to things like drugs, which at least provide short-term pleasure.

In truth, any substance that affects your brain state can be highly addictive. For example, studies show that when soldiers return from war, they are much more likely to engage in life-threatening behavior. Veterans of the Iraq and Afghanistan wars have a 75 percent higher rate of fatal motor vehicle accidents than civilians. Many of them are simply addicted to the enhanced feelings of presence they have in the combat zone.

If the living nightmare of war has addictive qualities, our mobile devices certainly can as well. That's because addiction is not about pleasure. It's about homeostasis: your body and brain like to stay in the state they are in. We are addicted to low levels of stress and the corresponding hormonal composition of our bodies. It's not that we like adrenaline and cortisol; it's that change is hard at both a conscious and a physiological level.

We don't look at our mobile devices ten times an hour because it's necessary. We look at them because we're addicts. In fact, in a recent deprivation study, researchers asked 1,000 students to not use their phone for a week. Half of the subjects quit the study within a day. Among the half that didn't, many reported physically shaking and compared themselves to "crackheads."

I can't teach you how to break your addiction. In fact, I don't think you really can. It's unrealistic to ask you to keep your phone on you and not to use it. It's like asking a cocaine addict to snort less cocaine. But you can manage it.

The answer is to leverage specific behaviors that reduce your digital exposure, ultimately training your brain like an athlete trains her muscles.

Make a binary life for yourself: part of it with device, part of it without. Structure times in the day when you don't have your phone on you. Lock it away in a closet when you get home where you can't see it. Keep it the hell away from your bedroom. Don't take it with you on the weekend.

Interruptions may seem innocuous, but they are sending nonstop jabs to the brain. They crush creativity. Research proves that an interruption forces a task to take 50 percent longer to complete and results in 50 percent more errors. It's not just our creativity being affected; it's our productivity.

Second, take breaks from digital technology. Studies prove that time in nature is critical for more than just creativity. It is critical for overall emotional health. In fact, Japanese researchers found that as little as 40 minutes in nature every week reduces ADHD by at least 50 percent.

Time in nature also increases overall happiness by releasing oxytocin into the brain. This hormone is cognitive fuel. It's typically released by the greatest things in life: sex, hugs and Jimmy Page guitar solos. It's proven to help create neural pathways in the prefrontal cortex. It helps form memories. It helps us produce great ideas.

Third, learn new skills. Believe it or not, we have a way to measure creativity called the Torrance Tests of Creative Thinking (TTCT). Using it, researchers have repeatedly found a direct correlation between learning new skills and overall creative output. It creates cognitive synergies. Your creativity will be more than simply the sum of your skills.

Of course, digital devices are absolutely critical to success in today's world. I'm not advocating for complete abandonment. We need to benefit from the positive aspects of technology while managing the negative.

In business, we are constantly looking for a competitive advantage. We cling to our mobile devices in an effort to be informed and connected. But our mobile addiction has a severe negative impact.

The moments you spend without your digital device—be it because you're with your family, going for a walk, playing guitar or simply disconnecting—are, in fact, some of the most important times for making you productive at work.

You're not cheating on your career when you're with your family. You're not cheating on your career when you are exercising or learning new skills. In fact, what you're doing is managing your career, because you're enabling your brain to be healthy, which will put you at peak performance.

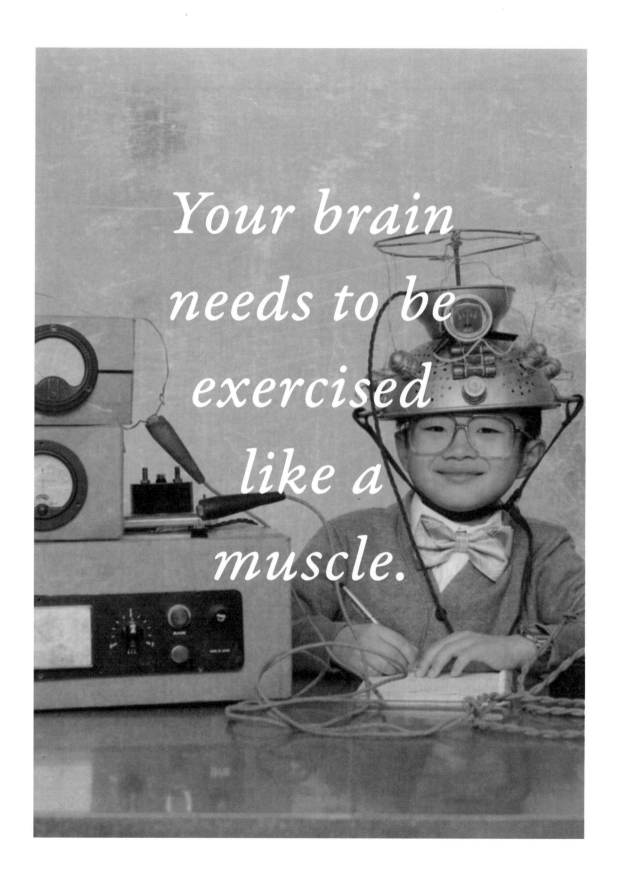

Your brain needs to be exercised like a muscle.

The power of alpha waves.

On May 6, 1965, Keith Richards did the one thing he was better at than playing guitar. He partied like a rock star.

In the early morning, Keith woke up with a melody in his head. He grabbed his guitar, pressed a button on his portable cassette recorder, played a few bars and passed out again.

Bedroom smartphone usage turns off the most powerful form of neurological creativity we have.

When he woke up, he found one of the most influential guitar riffs of all time waiting for him on tape. Followed, of course, by 40 minutes of him snoring because he didn't hit the stop button on the recorder.

The guitar riff served as the foundation for "(I Can't Get No) Satisfaction." The Rolling Stones recorded it using Keith's now signature fuzzbox on his guitar, which created a sound that Keith initially envisioned as a placeholder for a horn section. Three decades later, Rolling Stone magazine named it one the greatest pop songs of all time.

Keith was not alone in sleeping his way to a breakthrough. Late in 1963, Paul McCartney woke up with a melody in his head and wrote a song with the lyrics, "Scrambled eggs, Oh you've got such lovely legs, Scrambled eggs. Oh, my baby, how I love your legs."

The song seemed so familiar to Paul that he thought somebody else had already written it. He played it incessantly to other musicians and composers to ensure he didn't unintentionally poach it from another songwriter. Eventually, he realized it was his original composition and worked with

John Lennon to change the lyrics. The song became "Yesterday." Like "Satisfaction," it went on to be recognized as the one of the greatest pop songs of all time.

Waking up with a creative epiphany is not limited to rock stars. Dmitri Mendeleev, who looked like a prototypical mad scientist, was once a man obsessed with finding a way to organize the elements. In February 1869, he fell asleep while playing solitaire and woke up with the periodic table in his head. His table organized the elements in groups of seven, which, incidentally, is how solitaire is played. Numerous other scientific breakthroughs notably came from scientists when they first woke up, including the shape of DNA.

These early morning breakthroughs come from the brain's alpha waves, which are available to us during times of relaxation. They're one of the reasons we get so many great ideas when taking a hot shower. The philosopher and mathematician Descartes, famous for his statement, "I think, therefore I am," spent all morning drowsing, and he's generally recognized as one of the greatest thinkers of all time.

The problem is that the majority of us severely hamper our ability to create alpha waves. 71 percent of us sleep with our smartphones at our bedside. Half of us check it first thing in the morning or if they wake in the middle of the night. One third of us report that it's the most important priority when we wake up.

The impact of our bedroom smartphone usage is profound. When we use our phones, it kicks our fight-or-flight system into gear. It shuts down our alpha waves. It turns off the most powerful form of neurological creativity we have.

Of all the advice I have garnered and shared while writing the book, the one that has elicited the most positive feedback is this: feed your creativity first thing in the morning. Do not allow mobile devices into your bedroom. When you wake up, avoid them. Close your eyes. Relax. Then do something creative.

It doesn't matter what your creative love is. Play guitar, write poetry, build Legos with your kids or simply space out. Those early morning alpha waves are incredibly powerful. Perhaps more importantly, early morning creativity activates key areas of your brain, such as the prefrontal cortex, and reduces creativity-impeding chemicals such as adrenaline and cortisol. So it's not just about the initial benefits. Early morning creativity can affect your brain's creative performance for the entire day.

Feeding your creativity doesn't take long, and you don't need to be a candle-lighting yogi. Just spend 15 minutes every day. Your phone will be waiting for you when you are done— as will all of the social and business stresses that come with it.

7.3

Creativity really is like a muscle.

London doesn't have numbered or ordered streets like Paris or New York. Instead, its streets are a complex mess of curves, shortcuts and dead ends. As a result, being a cabbie in London is a respected profession, and to become one you have to master something called The Knowledge. It is a geography exam that covers the most efficient routes through London and all of the points of interest along them.

Over time, the areas of our brain that respond to the stress of interruptions grow while those that manage creativity shrink.

To pass the test, a driver is given two locations and must, without looking at a map, instantly recite the fastest route and everything along the way, down to the specific sequence of large hotels on a street. Not surprisingly, it takes months of training to do this, and around half of all candidates fail.

Neuroscientist Eleanor Maguire wanted to understand what mastering The Knowledge did to the shape of the brain. To do so, she studied aspiring taxi drivers and divided them into three groups: a control group, failed students and successful candidates.

What she found was amazing. She measured the posterior hippocampus, which is the area of the brain that manages spatial relations. It turned out to be larger than normal among the successful cab drivers. It had responded to repeated stimulus and grown like a bicep doing curls.

The analysis showed that like our bodies, our brains are extremely dynamic. They have a high degree of plasticity. They change quickly based on the stimuli we provide. Over time, we can make significant changes to our brain.

Maguire also found something alarming. A region near the posterior hippocampus called the anterior hippocampus shrank to make room for the growing region. Because the head creates a zero-sum game due to the fixed size of our skulls, one area had to give up space so another area could grow.

The seemingly lame analogy that compares brains to muscles is actually very accurate. The more we exercise specific regions, the more we build them up. The more we ignore specific regions, the more they atrophy.

Now let's think about our brains on digital devices. Like the London taxi drivers, we are growing some regions and shrinking others. When we constantly attack ourselves with digital information, we train our brains. Over time, the areas of our brain that respond to the stress of interruptions grow, while those that manage creativity shrink. It's not just about the short-term effects of interruptions, it's about the near-permanent changes it can make to our brains.

Changing behavior is hard.